Small Steps, Big Changes

Eight Essential Practices for Transforming Schools Through Mathematics

Pattern is a powerful teacher. In this timely book we see purposeful patterns that guide and sustain high levels of performance in elementary mathematics learning. What students talk about in math lessons and how they talk about it matters greatly. To develop thoughtful students who are tenacious and confident problem solvers requires teachers who model these same attributes in their work with students and with their colleagues. One exceptional teacher working in isolation does not have enough impact to affect students' deep understandings, skills, and identities as math learners. Our children deserve great math teachers and great math learning environments every year they are in school. By engaging the whole staff, Chris Confer and Marco Ramirez show you how to create a culture of ongoing student success in mathematics.

—*Bruce Wellman, codirector, MiraVia LLC, Guilford, Vermont*

"Small steps" do lead to "big changes"! The authors' approach has, indeed, transformed our school's mathematics. Our in-depth analysis of student work allowed us to identify "quality work" for each big mathematical idea in our grade level. The beauty of beginning with this end in mind is that this dynamic process creates clear pathways for children.

—*Amy McDonald, first-grade teacher, Warren Elementary School, Tucson, Arizona*

How does a school administrator with the best of intentions move a school forward in the area of math? This has been my question and goal for the past two years. *Small Steps, Big Changes* has offered us a process that focuses on student work and student thinking. We are witnessing student growth in their overall level of understanding of math concepts. The bonus is that teachers are growing in the areas of teaching and understanding math concepts along with the students.

—*Robin Dunbar, principal, Warren Elementary School, Tucson, Arizona*

Reading *Small Steps, Big Changes* is almost as good as having the authors working in your school. This very readable book is based on real situations, real student work, and real conversations with students and teachers.

Small Steps, Big Changes operates on the premise that, for high-poverty children, "schools are the main hope, perhaps the only hope." The suggestions for mathematics instruction are rigorous, engaging, and imminently doable. Every professional should have this book on his or her shelf!

—*Hulet E. Kitterman, principal, Louisville Academy, Louisville, Georgia*

From the big picture of schoolwide goals to the specificity of key concepts and skills, *Small Steps, Big Changes* provides a clear road map of the interdependent roles and responsibilities of administrators, coaches, and teachers but always through the filter of what it takes to guarantee short- and long-term progress for all students as mathematicians.

Marco Ramirez and Chris Confer open an exciting window for us to finally understand a school-based approach to research-based policies and practices that have achieved extraordinary results. Learn to ask the right questions, crystallize the core beliefs of your school, and focus on the high-benefit activities that create a school culture permeated with mathematical confidence and achievement.

—*Jane Foley, PhD, senior vice president, Milken Educator Awards, Milken Family Foundation*

Small Steps, Big Changes is an excellent example of how one school builds a culture of collective accountability and responsibility for deepening the understanding of mathematics instruction. This book provides us with a school-based perspective on how to create sustainable improvements in student learning of mathematics. The processes and practices used to transform this school provide administrators and teachers with a viable road map for working toward the implementation of the Common Core.

—*Steve Holmes, assistant superintendent, Sunnyside Unified School District, Tucson, Arizona*

Small Steps, Big Changes

Eight Essential Practices for Transforming Schools Through Mathematics

Chris Confer & Marco Ramirez
Foreword by Steven Leinwand

Stenhouse
PUBLISHERS

Portland, Maine

Stenhouse Publishers
www.stenhouse.com

Library of Congress Cataloging-in-Publication Data

Confer, Chris.
    Small steps, big changes: eight essential practices for transforming schools through mathematics/Chris Confer and Marco Ramirez; foreword by Steven Leinwand.
                p. cm.
    ISBN 978-1-57110-813-5 (pbk.: alk. paper) -- ISBN 978-1-57110-948-4 (ebook) 1. Mathematics--Study and teaching (Elementary)--United States. 2. School improvement programs--United States. 3. Motivation in education--United States. I. Ramirez, Marco. II. Title.
    QA135.6.C653 2012
    372.7--dc23
                                                                    2011041219

Cover design, interior design, and typesetting by designboy Creative Group.

Manufactured in the United States of America

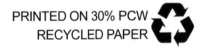

PRINTED ON 30% PCW
    RECYCLED PAPER

18 17 16 15 14 13 12 9 8 7 6 5 4 3 2 1

To David, who has supported me every step of the way.

—Chris

To my mother and father, Annabelle and Hector (Kuny) Ramirez, who have continued to influence and guide me, even though they have long passed from this life.

—Marco

Contents

Foreword

All those involved in trying to raise student achievement in mathematics know that traditional show-and-tell approaches—those that focus primarily on remembering how to get right answers to exercises—are not adequate. Such lessons cannot ensure the broad and deep mathematical understanding that is required of all students if they are to leave school ready for college and careers. That is why the spirit of the evolution from the NCTM Standards to the array of NSF-funded reform programs to the current focus on the coherent learning progressions of the Common Core State Standards for Mathematics is so vital to implement, yet such a challenge to cultivate and sustain. It is also why this wonderfully personal (yet easily generalized) tale of Chris Confer and Marco Ramirez's success provides so many essential lessons for launching, nurturing, and sustaining the change process toward high-quality mathematics instruction.

Far from being a tale of just process and generality, Chris and Marco begin with a clear vision of ensuring that every student is able to think and reason effectively; solve problems accurately, flexibly, and efficiently; communicate clearly using mathematical language and representations; and demonstrate their skills and knowledge on assessments. Although these ideas are similar to what is already found, and too often ignored, in many schools, this book presents a set of eight essential actions that help breathe life into these goals and transform them from idle words to daily classroom realities. These actions then become essential components of the culture of the school—questioning, studying, focusing, and collaborating become hallmarks of the very ethos of professional interactions.

It is a tale of patience and hard work, rewarded with high achievement and much more positive attitudes about math among students and teachers. It is also a tale driven by powerful mind-sets about leadership. As one principal in the book explains, "Taking on the stance of a researcher calls me to wonder why people do what they do and to work to understand how others are thinking. Research reminds me about the importance of puzzling about how things can be better." We hear a principal and math coach recount, "How could we aspire to have students who were good problem solvers without encouraging teachers to do the same? We could not ask students to think and reason, and then require teachers to blindly march through a curriculum. And we could not chant 'absolute fidelity to the core' while asking students to make sense of mathematics."

Throughout this book, we learn from the firsthand experiences of a successful principal who regularly coteaches and incessantly asks questions of himself, his staff, and his students. And we learn from an incredibly dedicated and thoughtful math coach who builds trust, one teacher at a time, with nonjudgmental competence and empathetic support. We also observe a set of teachers embark on the gradual process of shifting beliefs, building confidence and capacity, modeling effective practices, and growing personally and professionally. We listen in on coplanning sessions; we witness the coteaching as well as the debriefing of this experience. We are presented with classroom vignettes that resonate with our own experiences. And we watch as small victories get transformed into sustainable improvements. In short, we are taken on a journey that shows us how to make a real and lasting—not just superficial and short-term—difference in the mathematical lives of students, teachers, and principals.

As schools across the country engage in the process of understanding and implementing the new Common Core State Standards for Mathematics, the lessons learned and presented here are insightful guides for supporting transitions to a deeper understanding of mathematics, consistent use of more cognitively demanding practices, and more broadly effective instruction. We see that these transitions are hard, but they are far from impossible. We see how problems that arise become opportunities for growth. We see that the overarching mind-set of "We're all in this together" breeds a dignified and collegial approach that honors the importance of the people who work in our schools.

When all is said and done, Chris and Marco challenge all of us to become problem solvers and researchers on behalf of students. They challenge us to adapt their tale of success to our own schools. And they challenge us to build our own sustainable communities of excellence that mathematically empower all of our students.

Steven Leinwand
American Institutes for Research

Acknowledgments

How have I been so blessed? I have been surrounded, professionally and personally, by wise and perceptive colleagues who have gently guided me, learned alongside me, challenged me, questioned me, and inspired me. I can only hope to model myself after my mentors, many of whom Marco Ramirez lists below. All of us in education really do "stand on the shoulders of giants." I can hope for nothing better than to pass their gifts on to others.

Children are extraordinary teachers, and they open my eyes and surprise me on a daily basis. The young ones remind me that the mathematics that seems simple to us can be an exciting mystery to them. Older students challenge me to keep mathematics relevant and meaningful—protesting, "Why are we doing this, Miss?" when it's not immediately obvious.

I have had the incredible good fortune to work with children across the nation, including African American children in the South, some of whom were recent refugees from Hurricane Katrina; Latino children in the Southwest; and children from across the globe in the melting pot of New York City. In particular, Native American children, families, and teachers have welcomed me into their worlds, and they have taught me more than I can say. All children keep me humble, for one size can never fit all.

Toby Gordon kept her faith in this project of writing "a book about everything," astutely asking the right questions at the right times, providing space to make sense for ourselves, and nudging us along when necessary. Certainly, Marco and I owe the very existence of this book to her. Chris Downey found words when they failed Marco and me, and the support staff at Stenhouse—including Nate Butler and Jay Kilburn—have proven to be capable and professional.

One of my life gifts has been learning, researching, debating, and reflecting with Marco Ramirez. A professional partner, life coach, and good friend, Marco continually challenges my thinking and makes the journey fun.

My daughter, Amanda, is a perceptive educator and an effective professional developer, and I watch her with pride and learn from her perspective. Some key ideas in this book we owe to her. My son, Jonathan, ever reminds me of the importance of my goals, and he offers sound encouragement and advice, for which I am grateful. My husband, David, accompanies me both literally and figuratively on my real and intellectual journeys. My father is supportive and ever present, as is my mother, who has passed on; when I write, her voice whispers in my ear. David's parents are like my own, and they lovingly cheer me on and up.

This book in particular owes its existence to teachers, principals, and coaches in Tucson, Arizona, and across the country, who have honored Marco and me with their soul-searching reflections, insights, frustrations, and joys. Some of these colleagues Marco names below. Karolyn, Beth, Dora, Sam, Esther, Jaye, Ana, Cassie, and Kristina: you are a gift to education and to the children of Pueblo Gardens Elementary School. Brenda Whitehorse, Shawn Walbecq, and the teachers at Aneth Community School; Mia Toya and Debbie Scruggs; Phyllis Burks, Bam Miller, Nora Ramirez, Heidi Aranda, Connie Lewis, Kay Thill, Jackie Wortman, Olga Torres, and, of course, Carol Brooks—I have learned from all of you. Thank you!

Chris Confer

This book acknowledges the collective wisdom and experiences of all the truly magnificent people who have touched my life as an educator. Special thanks have to be given to the wonderful staff of Pueblo Gardens Elementary School, who traveled a journey that few were willing to take at the time, for the trust and support they have given me over the years that has made a difference in our professional lives and in the lives of our children. Special thanks to Dora Saldamando, Karolyn Williams, Elizabeth Egan, Cassie Gribble, Sam Luna, Jaye Downing, Ana Franco, Esther Guillen, and Kristina Rodriguez-Loya, who dared to research with Chris and me the depths of leadership, mathematics, and student success for more than a decade.

To the wonderful teachers and staff at Louisville Academy in Louisville, Georgia, for their dedication to changing how they teach mathematics, and for the success they achieved. Special thanks to Hulet Kitterman, principal of Louisville Academy, for her leadership and dedication to changing how mathematics is taught throughout her school.

To the many districts, principals, teachers, and schools where we have worked, we are forever grateful for the trust and support that you have given us. Your children have provided the evidence we needed to see that the work has made a difference in the students' mathematical success. It has been a privilege to work with you and your children. The work you've done has made a sustainable difference.

Over the years, several brilliant people have influenced Chris's and my thinking beyond measure in the areas of leadership and mathematics. The mathematical conversations we have conducted for over a decade with gifted mathematical minds such as Marilyn Burns, Nicholas Branca, Katherine Kharas, Ruth Parker, Constance Kamii, Nora Ramirez, and Catherine Fosnot have affected my own education and teaching of mathematics. Bruce Wellman, Carol Brooks, James Fish, Marla Motove, and Patti Lopez have been foundational contributors to Chris's and my rethinking about educational leadership and its successful application in schools of high poverty.

To my dear colleague and friend Chris Confer, I am blessed to have known and worked with you for nearly two decades. The mathematical conversations, debates, and educational challenges that we've shared have helped us bring this book to life. Your ability to put into words the work we have done over this time has been a true gift to me. I look forward to many more years of mathematical research and friendship.

There are those who, without knowing it, move us. The works of Eckhart Tolle and Stephen Covey continually beckon me to lead with integrity and presence. Becoming conscious in the work we do and the life we live is no small feat. For me, it will be a lifetime endeavor. Thank you both for the work you have done. It has made a difference for me and for children in schools.

To our editor, Toby Gordon, thank you for pushing ever so gently but methodically. Your insights into the world of mathematics are spot on. I appreciate your pushing us to create DVDs as another way of representing the work we do. I had always heard wonderful things about how you support your authors, but the experience was more profound than what I had imagined.

For every endeavor, there is a price to pay. For me, it was not being as present as a father and husband—soccer games were missed, fewer events were attended, and there were lapses in divine moments for conversation. To my wife, Julie, and my children, Claire, Elise, and David, I am ever so grateful for the support and understanding that you have given me these past two years, as time has not been an ally. I am eternally grateful and indebted to you all. To Julie, you have been foundational in keeping our lives afloat, and I appreciate all the extra work you did as a result of my absence. Know that you are always loved, even from afar.

Marco Ramirez

Introduction

A tale describes an old man digging frantically in the night,
the ground illuminated by a lantern on the wall in front of his house.
"What are you looking for?" inquired a friend.
"The gold coin that I lost," replied the old man.
"How did you lose it?" asked his friend.
"I lost it while working behind my house," he said.
"Then why are you looking for it in the front?" wondered the friend.
"Because there's enough light to dig here," answered the man.

For years and years we—Chris Confer and Marco Ramirez—worked as math resource teachers in high-poverty schools in Tucson, Arizona. We often worked together in a handful of schools where we provided mathematics professional development, workshops, and coaching for amazing, hardworking teachers. Like the old man above, we all were searching for that elusive gold coin: a school filled with confident students who could solve mathematics problems, saying, "That's easy! I can do that . . . and a whole lot more!"

Yes, good things happened in many of our schools. Over and over again we would see high-quality mathematics bubble up—for example, when a grade-level team at one school taught problem solving, or a group of teachers in another school used manipulatives to teach geometry. Children and teachers became excited and hopes would rise. "It really is possible!" we said.

But one by one these fragile bubbles popped before our eyes, for reasons as different as the schools where we worked. Perhaps teachers would change grade levels, or a principal would be reassigned. Hard work would dissipate into wisps of mist, and we found ourselves beginning the process all over again.

Does this story sound familiar to you? Many teachers, principals, and support people work to the point of exhaustion. They attend meeting after meeting, analyze standards, and write curriculum maps. They align instruction horizontally within grades and vertically between grades. They examine data of all kinds, arrive early at school and stay late, teach, and reteach . . . and in the end, test scores and classroom performance often show only incremental improvement.

Just like the old man in the story above, educators often seem to be digging in the wrong place.

Although the above school improvement strategies can be helpful, they are never sufficient. It is important for educators to set their sights on new, perhaps out-of-the-way places, where the gold actually lies.

Through the school-based research that we have done for nearly two decades, it is clear that all children—even English language learners and children who live in poverty—can succeed in mathematics. For principals, coaches, and teachers across the country the ultimate question remains: What does it take?

° What does it take for the majority of the students in any school to be successful in mathematics?

° And then, what does it take to sustain the success?

We have explored these questions for several decades in many schools in different states. Over time we compiled and adapted school reform and cross-curricular instructional strategies that pay off big dividends in mathematics. Over time we consulted in schools across the country, developed more mathematics program improvement strategies, and discovered how to adjust them for different populations of students and teachers.

In a school in the Tucson Unified School District, we brought together these mathematics program improvement strategies. Building on the work that the previous principal had done to bring together the community, we—Marco as principal, and Chris as instructional coach—worked alongside a group of hardworking teachers. Together we moved a school from "underperforming" to "highly performing" in mathematics in 2004–2005. Pueblo Gardens Elementary School, where about 94 percent of the students were at the poverty level and spoke five different languages at home, had 93 percent of its students meeting or exceeding state standards in third-grade mathematics. Over time other grades scored at high levels. And once the test scores rose, they remained at high levels.

Pueblo Gardens Elementary School, which once was looked down upon by many educators in the district, became an example of success. This high-poverty school with many English language learners hosted districtwide professional development sessions that showcased what their students could do. As a result, students in this high-poverty school helped teachers from other schools—even affluent schools—realize what high-quality student thinking looks like and sounds like. Consequently, many schools across the district adopted new strategies and benefited.

Most compelling, however, has been watching children become transformed, not only at Pueblo Gardens Elementary School, but at other schools where we have worked. Students learn to confidently solve problems in more than one way. They speak the language of mathematics. And most important, they love math.

Is this simple to do? *No.*

Is this a silver bullet, an easy cure-all? *No.*

But can other schools do the same? *Absolutely.*

We have learned that making sense of mathematics can change the culture of a school and sustain it. We have learned that quality patterns of teaching allow educators to work smarter rather than harder. We have learned that teachers, coaches, and principals who intertwine their roles and together research math instruction realize what is possible for children to achieve.

The Structure of This Book

Each chapter of our book outlines an essential idea that guides our work as we support schools. Each essential idea is clear, doable, and practical; we truly believe that significant change is within the reach of every school.

Each chapter ends with three stories that reflect the essential idea through three voices: the voice of a principal, the voice of a coach, and the voice of a teacher. The stories in this book describe the tools that we have used to help schools carve out their own unique paths to similar destinations.

No story in this book is that of a specific school, educator, or student with whom we have worked; we appreciate the trust that educators have offered us and respect the confidentiality that allows all of us to do our best. Each story, however, rings true because principals, coaches, and teachers across the country have surprisingly similar struggles, issues, and challenges. Each story reflects the common concerns, perspectives, and insights of hardworking, dedicated educators who truly want the best for their students.

We offer these ideas in the hope that they may help principals, coaches, and teachers release the potential that lies within each student—and each other. We know that success is possible when educators search for that gold coin in a different place. Without a doubt, abundant possibilities surround us all.

Chris Confer and Marco Ramirez
Tucson, Arizona
March 2011

Chapter 1
Keep the End in Mind

You must be the change you want to see in the world.

—Mahatma Gandhi

Schools, mathematics, and children are our all-consuming passion. We are consultants who embed our lives in schools, working with children, to "be the change" that we want to see. While supporting principals, coaches, and teachers, we keep an eye on the future's horizon, to glimpse the world where our children will someday live and, ideally, thrive.

Spin the clock backward in time to the 1950s and imagine schools in black-and-white images: desks in rows, students listening to lectures, and blackboards and work-book pages filled with computations. No wonder—at that time, adults needed basic skills in computation and literacy to do repeated tasks, jobs that are now completed in nanoseconds with computers and technology. Think back to the United States and its post–World War II society: more localized, predictable, and structured than today's global, wildly shifting, interdependent economy. The mathematics of the 1950s—its cousin "arithmetic"—served that era but is not sufficient for this one.

Today the Common Core State Standards for Mathematics have redefined our goals, mirroring the new needs of the twenty-first century. While maintaining important focus on core content and skill fluency, the CCSS also include practices such as reasoning, problem solving, perseverance, and justification, as well as application and understanding of concepts. "Being the change" requires educators to step in this new direction, shift their thinking . . . and make a journey.

The End in Mind

Say you plan a family trip: the first thing you agree on is the destination. You might consider driving from Maine to Miami along the shoreline to enjoy the view. Or maybe you'll consider driving through Norfolk, Virginia, for your favorite coconut cake at the No Frill Bar and Grill. Doesn't matter much, because you know that driving south will get you to your destination. Everyone agrees where Miami is.

However, even within a single school, hardworking educators aim for mathematical destinations as different as Des Moines, Los Angeles, and Paris—all at the same time.

Although common standards and common assessments are an important beginning, mathematics instruction will change significantly when principals, coaches, and teachers agree on what standards and mathematical practices look like in the classroom: What does high-quality work and thinking look like and sound like? What does it take to accomplish the standards?

Educators use common words—in very different ways. What does *rigor* mean from classroom to classroom?

° Pages filled with problems?
° Doing fifth-grade mathematics in fourth grade?
° Using different approaches or tools when solving problems?

And what does *problem solving* mean?

° Teachers guiding students through problem-solving steps?
° Students finding a correct answer to a word problem? . . . to multistep problems? . . . to problems that cross Common Core domains and clusters? . . . to complex real-world problems with more than one answer?

Most important, what one teacher considers high-quality work varies greatly from what the teacher next door considers high-quality work (see Figure 1.1). Of course, students are adaptable, and they quickly figure out how to get an A from a particular teacher. But "learning the teacher" cannot substitute for learning mathematics.

Mr. Westmoreland gives his fourth graders packets of math problems that students solve alone. When you walk into his classroom, it is usually silent, and you see Mr. Westmoreland moving from student to student, quietly correcting errors. Ms. Saenz has her fourth graders solve problems in groups of four. Her classroom is noisy, and her colleague across the hall sees her classroom as "chaotic."

One year, the principal held Mr. Westmoreland up to the staff as having an exemplary classroom, and the coach worried about Ms. Saenz's "lack of focus." The next year,

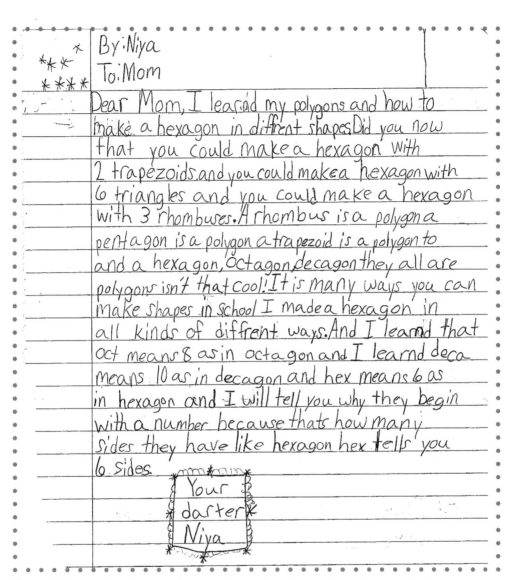

Figure 1.1 A second grader in a high-poverty school fills her mathematics journal with academic vocabulary and language.

a new principal praised Ms. Saenz's emphasis on cooperative learning, and the instructional coach encouraged Mr. Westmoreland to stop teaching through pages filled with calculation problems.

What is high-quality student work in mathematics? This question must be answered first. Once they agree on a destination, educators can discuss how they are going to get there.

When we begin our work at a new school, our first step is to ask the teachers, the coach, and the principal to bring samples of "high-quality student work" to a meeting. The differences in what the educators bring can be eye-opening.

Mr. Westmoreland brought to the meeting a sheet of fifty problems that a student, Gerard, had completed neatly with no errors. "Gerard is my best student," he told the group. "And I only had to tell him how to make common denominators once."

In contrast, Ms. Saenz brought a group poster that her students had made, showing how they identified equivalent fractions using paper fraction pieces.

As the coach, the principal, and the teachers examined the student work, the discussion—led by a protocol—took an interesting turn. "I like Gerard's neatness," Ms. Saenz commented, "and he certainly can multiply the numerator and denominator by the same number. But," she mused, "I can't tell whether he knows what equivalency means."

Ms. Saenz's work brought forward other comments: "I like the idea of cooperative work," Mr. Westmoreland said, "but I wonder whether all the students in the group understand what is on the paper. And the students won't have those pieces when they take the test. Don't they have to be able to solve the problem by making common denominators?"

"Ah," we thought as we once again recognized a group taking that crucial first step—educators uniting around a common concern, asking the important question: "What *should* our 'end in mind' be?"

Goals for Students

When we begin our work in any school, our goal is for its students, regardless of their socioeconomic status, to be mathematically competitive with other students in the United States. And we understand at a deep level that in this global, technological, mathematically based economy, all students—even those who may never have traveled outside their state—will one day have to compete for jobs with their peers in Japan or India or anywhere else in the world.

These are the goals for students that we promote and that many schools ultimately identify:
° Think and reason effectively
° Solve problems accurately, flexibly, and efficiently
° Communicate clearly using mathematical language and representations
° Demonstrate skills and knowledge on performance assessments as well as standardized tests

Think and Reason Effectively

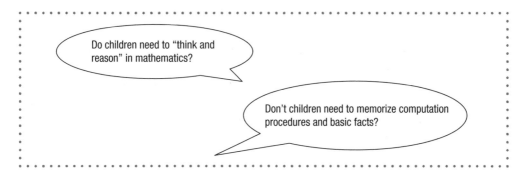

Figure 1.2

Answering the questions in Figure 1.2 honestly and directly is enormously important from the start. Educators and the American public are well aware that silver bullets and bandwagons abound, throwing the baby out with the bathwater and leaving children dripping in the puddles that remain. Leaving these questions unanswered derails countless mathematics improvement programs and muddies innumerable professional conversations.

We begin our work at all schools by confronting these two important questions. And we make clear that the answer to both questions must be a resounding "Yes!"

° Yes, children must think and reason, and make sense of mathematics—in the same way that they comprehend text when reading.

° And, yes, children must become efficient with skills and procedures—in the same way that they become fluent readers.

Our goal is always to have a balanced approach to mathematics, to make sure that the pendulum gently sways in the middle around sense-making. Extremist pendulum swings serve no one—certainly not the children. From the start of any school improvement relationship, we make it abundantly clear that fluent skills *and* understanding of concepts are important. The Common Core State Standards also make this connection explicit.

Mathematics must be a tool that children and adults can use to accurately solve problems. Otherwise algorithms and skills lie dormant in the classroom, or even worse, they are applied incorrectly. And children—especially children of poverty—may have less motivation to memorize material that is not useful or obviously applicable in their lives.

In contrast, when children are invited to use their skills and knowledge to solve interesting problems, mathematics becomes an exciting and lively puzzle. And when students understand the purpose for learning basic facts, they are more likely to make the effort.

Keeping the balanced approach clear from the start defuses teacher and parental anxiety, and most of all, is an accurate portrayal of what mathematics is. Yes, students will develop conceptual understanding. And, yes, students will learn their basic facts and computation. Most important, children who have both abilities can become capable, competent, and confident.

Figure 1.3 is the visual reminder that we use to model the intersection of thinking and reasoning, problem solving, and efficient skill development that guides all of our work. This graphic remains in the forefront of all discussions about improving mathematics, to continually highlight the critical role of both conceptual understanding and skill fluency in problem solving.

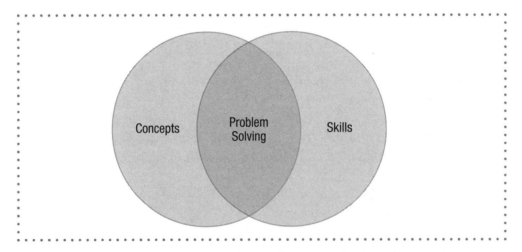

Figure 1.3 Both concepts and skill fluency are necessary for students to become effective problem solvers.

James Hiebert (1997) explains the importance of conceptual development this way:

Knowing mathematics, really knowing it, means understanding it. When we memorize rules for moving symbols around on paper, we may be learning something, but we are not learning mathematics. When we memorize names and dates we are not learning history; when we memorize titles of books and authors we are not learning literature. Knowing a subject means getting inside it and seeing how things work, how things are related to each other, and why they work like they do. (Hiebert et al., 2)

How typical throughout the United States is mathematics instruction that focuses on both skills and concepts? Do teachers usually help students understand mathematics and make connections? Studies that compare student achievement in the United States with student achievement in other countries around the globe consistently result in U.S. students scoring about average, rather than at a high level.

James W. Stigler, James Hiebert, and a team of specialists analyzed videotapes from the Third International Mathematics and Science Study 1995 (TIMSS) from eighth-grade classrooms in Japan, Germany, and the United States. The results led them to make the following conclusion about the United States:

The level is less advanced and requires much less mathematical reasoning than in the other two countries. Teachers present definitions of terms and demonstrate procedures for solving specific problems. Students are then asked to memorize the definitions and practice the procedures. In the United States, the motto is "learning terms and practicing procedures." (1999, 27)

In Stigler and Hiebert's 1999 study of classroom videos made during the 1995 TIMSS, the analysis included coding the problems twice: first for the kind of problem and second for how the problem was implemented, or presented to students, in classrooms.

In the United States, teachers implemented none of the *making connections* problems in the way in which they were intended. Instead, the U.S. teachers turned most of the problems into procedural exercises or just supplied students with the answers to the problems. (Stigler and Hiebert 2004, 15)

For example, Teacher A might provide students with a number of different triangles drawn on grid paper and have students figure out a method for finding their areas. In contrast Teacher B might simply tell the students the formula for finding the area of triangles: "$\frac{1}{2}$ (base × height)." At first glance you might ask yourself, "What's wrong with this? That *is* the formula for the area of a triangle. Why should students have to struggle when you can just *tell* them?"

Telling students formulas may seem efficient. But more efficient is allowing students to see how triangles and rectangles relate to each other (see Figure 1.4). The formula for the area of a triangle—length times width divided by 2—has a basis in reality. When students make sense of this formula, they are more likely to remember it.

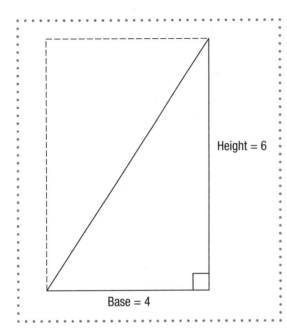

Height = 6

Base = 4

Figure 1.4 Area of a rectangle = base × height. Area of a triangle = $\frac{1}{2}$ base × height.

So why don't more teachers teach both skills and concepts? Few teachers have had the benefit of learning mathematics conceptually when they were children themselves. Teachers do the best they can and teach what they know.

The Common Core State Standards for Mathematics are merely the beginning. Standards are filtered through the teachers' lives and experiences. Teachers today are the "notch generation," because they are being asked to teach in a way that they never experienced as children. So although mathematics standards may be common, good mathematics experiences that illuminate these standards are uncommon. As a result, most schools find that professional development is critical for teachers as they journey through new, uncharted territory.

Solve Problems Accurately, Flexibly, and Efficiently

Problem solving is not a new idea for most educators—after all, childhood textbooks with word problems at the end of each chapter are indelibly ingrained in the memories of most adults. However, the role that problem solving should play in schools might surprise some people: problem solving is at the center of all instruction.

When students do computation, their thinking should be high-level, critical thinking—including the use of the same math strategies that many adults in the United States employ in their daily lives.

Try solving this problem:

You are shopping at a grocery store. You have a twenty-dollar bill in your pocket. You find a frozen pizza for $10.00, a bag of apples for $5.55, and a box of cereal for $4.65. Do you have enough money to buy everything?

When you solved this problem, did you do it mentally or use paper and pencil?

Juanita, a third grader, did mental math to answer this question in the same way that an adult shopper might:

> I looked at the dollars for what I want to buy first—and that's $19. Then I could see that inside 55 is 50 cents and inside 65 is another 50 cents, so things I want to buy cost more than my $20.

Peek into a high-quality mathematics class at any school and you'll be sure to find plenty of the kind of mental math that is so much a part of the world around us. However, you might be surprised to find that during a typical lesson, students might solve only a handful of written problems rather than the pages of problems that you remember from your childhood textbook.

Students approach each word problem in a problem-solving manner. You'll hear lots of talk, even debate, as they justify their thinking and correct their own mistakes. But best of all, you'll feel the energy of young minds engaged in the excitement of solving problems for themselves.

Callie's eyes shone excitedly:

> Look at it this way! I took 35 cents from the apple price and put it with the cereal's 65 cents and that costs another dollar. So I add up the dollars: 5 + 1 + 4 + 10. That's already $20 and I'd need $.20 more to buy everything.

She drew the sketch in Figure 1.5 so that Fabian could understand what she did:

But Fabian had a question for Callie. "I like how you made the cereal 5 dollars. That was cool! But how did you end up with 20 cents more? I got 25."

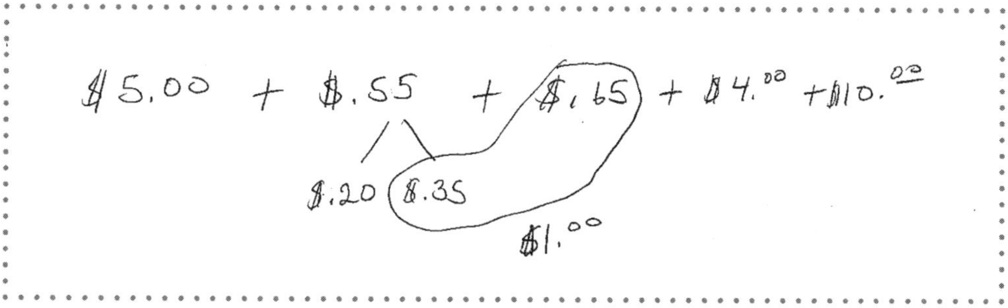

Figure 1.5 Callie made 65 cents into a dollar by taking 35 cents from the 55 cents.

This glimpse into a conversation between students illustrates the value that the Common Core State Standards for Mathematics bring to goals for students. Callie used the associative property of addition as an effective strategy, as opposed to simply memorizing this property. Common Core State Standards require students to use properties to solve problems and to understand and demonstrate understanding of place value. Furthermore, the Common Core Standards for Mathematical Practice, which describe student proficiencies beyond content, require students to justify their thinking in the way that Callie did.

Problem solving requires a degree of intellectual struggle. Good math problems make students want to do that kind of mental exercise. They make students dig into the recesses of their minds to bring to the surface all that they know that might help them solve the problem. Good math problems encourage students to think back to similar problems they've done in the past, and try out tools and models that could help them. Most important of all, intellectual struggle develops persistence.

Accuracy

Accuracy in problem solving is golden. Accuracy is the result of effective thinking and reasoning. Although there may be more than one right answer to a single problem, any correct answer has to be a reasonable answer for that specific problem. For example, a problem might be 27 ÷ 6.

Examine the following word problems, and consider these questions:
° Are all of the answers correct?
° How are the answers the same and different?

. . . .

1. A birthday party had 27 balloons, and 6 children got to share them equally. How many balloons did each child get?
2. A class of 27 students was going to the museum in 6 cars. How many students went in each car?
3. Amanda had a plate of 27 brownies to share evenly with 6 friends. How many did each friend get?

. . . .

1. *Answer: Each child got 4 balloons, and they gave the leftover balloons to the birthday boy.*
2. *Answer: There were 4 students in 5 cars, and 6 students in the other car.*
3. *Answer: $4\frac{1}{2}$ brownies*

Answers to problems often differ according to context. In each word problem the remainder was dealt with differently, and other possible answers exist: the leftover balloons could be popped, the number of cars depends on how many seat belts are in each car, and Amanda's friends might give her the leftover brownies.

Flexibility

Whenever we begin our work, one of the "ends" that we have in mind surprises some parents and teachers: students need to have more than one way to solve problems—even computation problems.

Multiple strategies help students develop a variety of powerful understandings about the number system, properties of numbers, and how operations relate to each other. High-caliber mathematics students call on their knowledge of mathematics properties and number relationships to deal effectively with mathematical problems. Students who are flexible thinkers are independent workers, and are not reliant upon the teacher. Flexible thinkers don't cry out the lament that is familiar to many teachers: "Do I add? Do I subtract? Just tell me what to do, and I'll do it." Instead, they confidently attack a problem and persist in trying alternative approaches if the first one does not work.

For example, a first grader may be given the problem 9 + 6. That child may use a counting strategy by collecting those numbers of items and counting them, or by drawing and counting pictures by ones.

Although counting strategies are useful for small numbers, and are typical and important for young children to learn to manage, they are not the end point. Another first grader solves the problem a different way. Examine Elise's strategy, and consider these questions:
° What does the child know?
° Why is this knowledge important?

. . . .

Elise said, "Hmm . . . 6 + 9. I know that
10 + 6 is 16, so
9 + 6 has to be 15."

. . . .

Elise uses the commutative property for addition; she knows that 9 + 6 will have the same answer as 6 + 9. Furthermore, she uses algebraic reasoning. She knows that 10 + 6 = 16, so she just subtracts 1 to get the answer. Elise's flexibility of thinking is a marker of her good number sense.

Efficiency

Learning takes time. The first video that we made on our computers was difficult, frustrating, and time-consuming. We worked by trial and error, we had to view the tutorials over and over, and we finally resorted to asking a teenager who was in the vicinity. Making the second video was less traumatic, and now we put together videos quickly without a problem.

Learning mathematical ideas takes time as well. However, we must keep the goal of efficiency in sight. We do not want students to check their change at the grocery store by saying, "Excuse me, ma'am, but I'm going to get my beans out of my pocket to see if you gave me the right coins." In the same way that fluency is clearly a goal for reading, fluency and efficiency must be clear goals for mathematics instruction.

Communicate Clearly Using Mathematical Language and Representations

Mathematics is a language. Just like Spanish, Japanese, or any other language, mathematics has its own vocabulary, its own syntax, and its own sign system or set of symbols. Consider this question from upper-level algebra:

. . . .

Identify how each map is a group homomorphism. What is its kernel?

. . . .

This question is clearly written in English. Although most adults will understand the everyday meanings of *map, group, and kernel,* their meanings in this context are specific to mathematics. Furthermore, the answer is written using symbols and syntax that are also unique to the language of mathematics.

To participate in classroom mathematics discussions, students must fluently comprehend and use the language of mathematics. When they are required to communicate their mathematical ideas, they clarify and revise their own thinking, and encounter the need to convince others. Equity—the aspiration that all students will be competent in mathematics—requires teachers to consider the needs of second language learners in a learning community. Mathematical representations such as number lines, ten frames, and fraction bars help make abstract ideas visible, and promote clear and precise communication in the classroom.

Pueblo Gardens Elementary School has many English language learners. Teachers in schools with high populations of English language learners must explicitly and consistently teach the language of mathematics, employing every language development tool they can find. Not only are mathematical language skills imperative to help all of our students be part of the mathematical learning community, but all students must be able to successfully navigate the mathematical language that is so much a part of standardized tests.

Demonstrate Skills and Knowledge on Performance Assessments as Well as Standardized Tests

When we began our work at Pueblo Gardens Elementary School, the school had been categorized as "underperforming," based on state standardized test scores. However, the state test had only multiple-choice questions, and required no writing and little critical thinking. Our goal was to have students perform at an even higher level on performance assessments, by solving problems in more than one way and by using mathematical terminology to explain their thinking. But one of our criteria for success was for students to be able to pass those multiple-choice, standardized state tests.

Over time, through a lot of work by a great group of dedicated staff members, this became a reality. We knew we were approaching our goals when third graders finished the standardized test and commented, "Is that all it was? We thought it would be harder!" Is this type of positive outcome unique to Pueblo Gardens? No—we've heard similar stories in other schools where we have worked.

Goals for Teachers

Goals for students will inevitably influence goals for teachers. Principals cannot ask students to think and reason, and then require teachers to blindly march through a curriculum. Professional development facilitators cannot require "absolute fidelity to the core" while asking that students be problem solvers.

Instead, teachers must be skilled practitioners who purposefully focus instruction on structured, engaging, high-level mathematics. Teachers must be clear about mathematical concepts, understand the pathway that students frequently take to get there, assess where students are along that pathway, and differentiate instruction and interventions accordingly.

As we began our work at Pueblo Gardens Elementary School, we felt strongly that teachers needed a high-quality reform-based mathematics program that would support these new goals, along with the best professional development possible. We knew that ultimately, they needed new tools to reach new goals. We all would have to continually re-create our own vision of what children are capable of in mathematics. At the same time, we knew that if our own preferred program did not yield high-level results, that program, too, would be reevaluated.

In the many schools where we work, we find that our biggest task is helping educators shift the outcomes that they keep in mind. Figure 1.6 summarizes these important shifts.

Conventional Wisdom	Shifting for Change
The "end" that we're aiming for is a child who can perform well on multiple-choice tests.	The "end" is a child who • thinks and reasons effectively; • solves problems accurately, flexibly, and efficiently; • communicates clearly using mathematical language and representations; and • demonstrates his or her knowledge and skills on performance assessments as well as standardized tests.
Most instruction should focus on memorization of traditional computational procedures and basic facts.	Instruction that balances concepts and skills is important. Both understanding and fluency with basic facts allow students to be effective problem solvers.
Focusing professional development on test scores has the largest payoff for improvement in school mathematics programs.	Focusing on high-quality student work has the largest payoff for improvement in school mathematics programs.

Figure 1.6 Productive shifts for mathematics improvement

Keep the "End in Mind"

Identifying the right destination for their mathematics program is the hardest and most important task that educators have. Principals, coaches, and teachers must identify what is right for our students, today, in our global, technologically based society.

Our "end in mind" is that students must be able to do the following:

1. Think and reason effectively
2. Solve problems accurately, flexibly, and efficiently
3. Communicate clearly using mathematical language and representations
4. Demonstrate their knowledge and skills on performance assessments as well as standardized tests

The road may be somewhat bumpy at times, but keeping focused will create a journey toward a school where students enjoy math because it makes sense to them, and where they travel a road that they understand. As teachers, coaches, and principals journey together, they come to understand their shared purpose and destination: mathematical success.

Throughout the nation, educators are working extremely hard. An enormous amount of time, energy, and money is being spent on mathematics reform. Aiming these resources in the right direction is the key.

Three Voices, One Purpose

New destinations require new journeys, which can be described most clearly in the voices of those on the path. We invite you to hear real stories from educators around the country about "keeping the end in mind," from the perspective of a principal, a coach, and a teacher.

The Principal's Perspective

Most of my administrative classes described the principal's first job: to create a mission and vision statement. By the end of our program, we could almost chant the ubiquitous mission and vision statement that underpinned every school improvement book that we read and each administrative professional development session:

"We are a school that promotes high achievement, twenty-first-century thinking skills, and a safe and caring environment that values diversity and cultural heritages."

"There it is again," I thought. "But exactly what does that statement mean?" I figured that there were as many different interpretations as there were people in the room—especially in mathematics, where many teachers were not confident in their own abilities, let alone able to help children improve.

I could tell that the staff at my new school needed to clarify the "end" that we had in mind for students. We needed to identify what high achievement in mathematics looks like. I was convinced that, although the teachers had a general idea, they had not clarified that as a school. I knew that this consistency would be especially important in a school with children of poverty. Years later we are still having this same discussion as we raise our understanding of what children can do in mathematics.

For the last several years, I've ended the year by asking the teachers to gather "high-quality work" in mathematics. That's all I've said; I've kept it somewhat ambiguous on purpose, to see what kind of student work the teachers really value.

Reviewing this work during Professional Learning Community meetings the following year has made for some powerful, even emotional, discussions. Teachers who have taught for a long time have to confront the idea that what they were chasing was only part of the story—that right answers and skills were important, but that there was still a lot more work to do. Other teachers have to confront other assumptions. Giving up what you believe strongly can be very challenging, especially when you're also under the gun from the state for low performance.

Early on at our school, I could see that teachers were pulling their lessons from a wide variety of places: from different Internet sites, from old workbooks, from books purchased at the local teaching materials store, and from the high-caliber series that the previous principal had purchased—but that they used only sporadically. I was clear that we needed to have a much more consistent approach to mathematics content if the children had any hope of catching up to their peers from higher socioeconomic levels.

I was also very aware that I needed to engage the teachers in thinking and reasoning, and that we would have a professional culture of research in the best possible sense. Researching would make teachers conscious of their instructional decisions and move the most effective choices into consistent patterns. And I needed to do this in more than just words: my actions had to mirror this as well. I decided that teacher research would drive all of our work. The value is respect for kids' intellect and capability—these kids can. The question that we had to research was, "What will it take?"

It wasn't easy. The teachers had to come to see that my mathematics research questions were honest ones, that I was learning how to teach math better myself. I told the staff that I was going to choose at least one classroom each year in which to teach mathematics lessons on a regular basis. And I did. Each year I chose one aspect of teaching to focus on, and I told the teachers that I was working on it. It made for great hallway discussions and great ways to bring up what I wanted them to research as well, and really made the evaluation process legitimate. After all, I had my own stories about helping Joaquin learn his combinations of ten, and about how surprised I was that Kayla couldn't use the number line and how that had caused me to question when and how we should use it.

Last year I worked a lot in Kelly's fourth-grade classroom. I chose her because she was new to our school and I would get a "double bang" out of my time by enculturating her into our school's value system while modeling lessons.

As we cotaught the lesson, Kelly and I quickly realized that we needed to talk less and have the students talk more throughout the lesson.

I worked that story into many of my conversations with teachers, especially those who could stand to be less of a "sage on the stage" and more of a facilitator. Over the year I honed my use of student engagement tools, such as partner talk, students revoicing big ideas, and using choral response.

Best of all, during staff meetings I told stories from my work with kids, stories that brought the staff and me to the same level, learning together about what it takes to help these kids be anything they want to be. And I have a legitimate place from which to speak during evaluations: I know what works. It's powerful stuff.

Through my own research I learned about patterns that made my work more efficient, and helped teachers bridge that gap between where they were and where they wanted to go. During our school's journey toward improved student achievement, we kept our "end," or vision of student competence, clearly in sight.

The Math Coach's Perspective

Whenever I begin coaching at a school, my first two goals are to build trust and to uncover the kind of student work that the teachers value.

Building trust is crucial. If I'm going to encourage teachers to think and reason about their mathematics instruction, they will have to take the risk of sharing their questions, concerns, and worries. Teachers don't merely have to open their classroom doors to me; they have to open their hearts and minds. And this can be difficult, because for many people, teaching is very personal work.

I have to be real about my own questions about teaching mathematics. I'm not perfect, I laugh at my mistakes, and I make plans to change things I do that don't go well. I model the kind of learner that I hope all teachers will be.

What is different about me is that I've had the chance to focus on math for a long time—one of my friends told me that I'm "pickled" in math! But even though I know a lot of math content and good teaching strategies, every day in the classroom poses new challenges for me.

Why did Serena easily count 35 cubes one day and then say that 11 is less than 9? Why did Julio, who sailed through our fractions menu, mark $\frac{3}{8}$ as larger than $\frac{3}{4}$ on his end-of-unit assessment? How should we adapt the multiplication unit for Amanda, who is mathematically talented? I think that my most effective work with teachers happens when I move from consultant mode, where I simply make suggestions to them, to collaborative, coteaching mode.

When I work with teachers, I have to respect their choices because they ultimately are responsible for their students' learning. One year some upper-grade teachers accepted my challenge to move to a reform-based, problem-solving curriculum. However, they were not comfortable giving up their traditional textbook.

For a while this team of teachers chose to double up on math time, teaching it for two periods a day, using their old textbook for one period and using the new curriculum for the other. I guess to them it felt like the right, perhaps safe, thing to do. I respected their choice and supported their work while asking the questions that a good researcher asks: What is the outcome of each program? Did doubling up on math time make a difference? What did we give up as a result?

My other beginning job as a math coach is to uncover how the teachers perceive high-quality work. I do this by helping them research two questions:

○   What are high-quality tasks?
○   What are high-quality student responses for those tasks?

I encourage the teachers to do preassessments at the beginning of the year and at the beginning of each unit. We discuss the assessments they have used in the past and how they have analyzed the results. I keep samples of their high-quality student work, to keep track of our increasing understanding of what high-quality work can be. Typically their high-quality work samples change a great deal the second year, in terms of both the tasks and how they approach the problems.

Often teacher assessments at first address only computation, and they count as correct only the traditional algorithm. This tells me that these teachers have probably had few opportunities to understand what number and operation sense is. I offer them additional problems to include on their tests or alternative assessments to use.

When teachers show me student writing that lacks mathematical terminology—for example, fifth graders writing *shape* instead of *polygon*—I know that we can easily increase expectations for students and use new strategies to incorporate mathematical vocabulary in instruction.

Over the course of the year, I ask teachers to bring two samples of high-quality work to schoolwide discussions, where teachers of different grade levels examine the work in depth. We often realize that we aren't aiming for the same goal. I learn along with the teachers that students can do much more than I ever dreamed. And, best of all, the sharing helps us understand how each grade builds collectively into children's total experience over their years at the school.

The Teacher's Perspective

I remember the principal coming in and telling me that he was going to teach in my class. I thought, "Yeah, right. What principal does that? He'll get busy with discipline in the office and I'll never see him." Was I ever in for a surprise.

He came in for math about once a week. And he either taught a lesson or jumped into what I was teaching, by asking questions I hadn't thought of or pointing out interesting ideas that the kids had—or misunderstandings that were out there. And, you know, the fact that he taught math made a big difference to the kids. They came to think that math was so important that even the principal taught it. It made them even more excited. Of course, he sometimes had the same problems I did in teaching—sometimes the kids didn't understand, or they got frustrated. It was really neat to have professional discussions with my principal. We did some good thinking together.

I remember having the math coach come in, and I thought, "Do I really need all this help? I think I'm doing just fine." Then she'd ask these questions, and I remember deciding, "This is where my thinking is. I'm willing to play with this and I'm not willing to give up on my kids. I want the best for them."

Now it's really interesting to look at the student work that I felt was high quality at the beginning. I can't believe the difference in what I'm asking kids to do today; the change is obvious. How I'm teaching kids must be dramatically different, too.

Figure 1.7 shows a piece of student work that I collected years ago:

I listed these characteristics that many years ago I thought made the papers high quality:

- ° Neat and easy to read
- ° Correct answer
- ° Use of the traditional procedure
- ° Words, numbers, and pictures explain student thinking

Figure 1.8 shows a piece of high-quality student work that I collected recently.

This is my new view about high-quality work:

- ° Correct, reasonable answer
- ° Neat and easy to read
- ° Problem solving that shows use of place value, number sense, and operation sense
- ° High-caliber mathematical vocabulary and mathematical language, diagrams that efficiently illustrate the idea being communicated

There are __44__ fish
I think this because ......
22 + 22 is 44.

Figure 1.7 A teacher's sample of "high-quality" student work from ten years ago

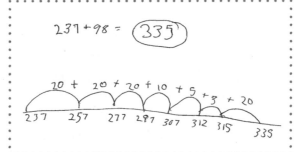

Figure 1.8 This recent sample of "high-quality" student work from the same teacher shows a higher level of student thinking and more awareness of number relationships.

I can see that even this high-quality work is not "there." To me, teaching is a journey. I'm in a different place today in my teaching, and I can only hope that ten years from now I'll see high-quality work from a perspective that has changed yet again.

Chapter 2
Understanding the Problem

If you do not change direction, you may end up where you are heading.

—Lao Tzu

A change of direction in mathematics is the goal. But how should schools adjust their sails? Which winds and currents can take them on that journey? And how can the people on the boat mobilize their unique talents to respond to inevitable waves and storms, as well as to the occasional smooth sailing?

The answers to these questions are as unique as the schools themselves. But if educators are to answer them effectively, they first must take the time to understand the problem. Typically schools identify problems, and then educators hurriedly come to solutions, many of which may not in reality help them achieve their goals. Haste is understandable—time is precious, money is scarce, and the problems schools face are many. However, first taking the time to understand a problem pays off in great dividends. Otherwise . . .

Mathematics programs are used for a few years, and then abandoned. "It didn't work," a coach explains.

School change structures are tried for a while and then eliminated. "Professional Learning Communities took too much time, and we didn't see many results," a teacher says.

Students begin to reason mathematically, but test scores improve only incrementally. "We didn't close the achievement gap," a principal observes.

Back in the classroom, understanding the problem is also an issue for students. They must learn that jumping to solutions to word problems before understanding what is being asked is a recipe for wrong answers:

There were 10 frogs by the pond. A dog barked. Some frogs jumped into the pond, but 2 frogs stayed on the shore. How many frogs jumped into the pond?

Jolene saw the 10 and the 2, decided to add the numbers, and quickly wrote, "12 frogs jumped in." She didn't take the time to reflect on what the problem was asking, and her answer did not make sense: more frogs jumped into the pond than were on the shore to begin with!

Making sense is key to effective problem solving for both students in the classroom and educators in the schools. A guiding principle for our work with schools is one that is sometimes attributed to Albert Einstein: "Understanding the problem is more important than finding a solution." But what does "understanding the problem" look like when working toward school change?

Understanding School Culture

Culture is one of the most misunderstood and underused leverage points in schools. If you randomly asked any three schools about their culture, the responses might sound something like this:

"We are a back-to-basics school."
"We believe that all children can learn."
"We are peacemakers."

When educators work within a culture, their cultural beliefs are often less evident than they might think. A school that lives and breathes the cultural notion of peace would have the teachers, principal, counselor, and staff organize their thinking around how to create peace throughout the day. What would this look like and sound like?

For example, a principal disciplining an unruly student could begin the conversation by saying, "Did your actions create peace? If not, how do you know? What could you do to build peace with the other children?"

Imagine everyone at a school using reflective peace-centered language with children at every turn:

"Did you use peaceful words during recess?"

"When you helped your friend who broke her pencil, you were creating peace."

"Marcie got really mad and pushed you. But you remained peaceful and didn't push her back. How did this help Marcie be more peaceful?"

In contrast, a "peacemaking" school might merely write a mission statement, place posters around the school encouraging students to be peaceful, and have an assembly about peace. It is the living of an idea, the operationalization of a belief, that shifts a school culture. Keeping a focus front and center, examining decisions through that lens, and talking about it on a regular basis in classrooms and in hallways is what makes cultures shift.

Even schools that seem to be clearly organized around a culture differ in how educators operationalize that culture. In a "back-to-basics" school, what does *basic* really mean? In one school a teacher showed the students many of what he called "shortcuts" or "tricks." Yet a different teacher defined *basic* as foundational concepts and skills. She valued both memorizing and having children use and apply mathematics in complex problems.

Creating cohesiveness, especially about what is important for students to learn in mathematics at each grade level, provides a huge leverage point from which a large amount of work and change can happen.

A School Culture of Mathematical Thinking

To check to see whether you have a school culture that values mathematical thinking, ask yourselves these questions:

Is making sense of mathematics the basis of nearly every mathematical discussion in classrooms and among teachers, the principal, and the coach? (See Figure 2.1.) Are educators clear about the importance of skills?

Do teachers consistently ask students to solve problems

Figure 2.1 An instructional coach and a first-grade teacher discuss how to help students make sense of more-complex word problems.

in two different ways, and to explain their thinking with diagrams, verbally, and numerically?

Do teachers and students consistently use words such as *flexibility* or *strategy, models,* and *efficiency*?

Does the student work match the culture being promoted? For example, to subtract 98 from 100 would a student use the traditional algorithm and "borrow" or simply add 2 to 98 to find the difference?

Student work is the best evidence of culture. Children have always been good at internalizing school cultures, and the work they produce reflects what the adults around them value. Many parents cringe at hearing a five-year-old play house when their own reprimands leave the dear child's lips word for word.

Ask children, "What are good ways of solving math problems?" Very few children are asked this powerful question in schools. You may be surprised to hear answers such as the following, which primary students actually gave us:

Think before you start.
Draw a picture to understand the problem.
Explain how you solved it, using the math vocabulary.
Check your work. Do it a different way.

Or your students might give answers like these:
Write the numbers straight.
Don't talk when you work. That's cheating.
Do it just like the teacher did.
Count on your fingers to check.

The first classroom mathematics culture clearly is focused on thinking and reasoning and mathematical communication. The second is a culture that promotes neatness, working alone, and repetition of a low-level procedure.

How often do we hear people in schools refer to the importance of "out of the box thinking" or "critical thinking"? Unfortunately many educators must learn what that looks like in mathematics, because they did not learn to solve problems in multiple ways when they were children in school. Many teachers don't know what computation strategies students can use beyond the traditional U.S. algorithm. Many schools find that they need outside professional development to gain the expertise that is lacking within. When teachers deepen their understanding of mathematics and how to support student learning, they can more quickly affect the students they have . . . here and now.

Here are some steps that help educators clarify problems and set their schools on the road toward workable solutions.

State the Problem

The word *problem* makes most educators shudder as they visualize their time disappearing into conflicts and conferences, meetings and piles of paperwork. We try to see problems in a different light: as simply the difference between today—the imperfect present—and our belief in what is possible.

We begin the mathematics change process by stating the actual, specific problem rather than a preconceived solution. When faced with an unsuccessful mathematics program, educators often state the problem by asking, "How can we improve our mathematics test scores?"

Focusing primarily on test scores will simply add another layer to the mass of failed mathematics program improvement projects. The reality is that low test scores are not the problem, but instead are a symptom of a problem. In the same way that both a sore throat and appendicitis can result in a fever, a variety of factors can make test scores suffer.

At our school, we began to understand the problem by specifically stating it using the "ends" that we had previously identified:

Our students need to

- think and reason effectively;
- solve problems accurately, flexibly, and efficiently;
- communicate clearly using mathematical language and representations; and
- demonstrate their knowledge and skills on performance assessments as well as standardized tests.

Gather Data

Yes, it is important to gather traditional summative data about state tests and widely used formative assessments such as benchmark tests and mathematics unit assessments. But important information awaits in informal conversations, student work, lesson observations, checklists of skill acquisition, systemic analysis tools, and other formative assessments.

Data from Informal Conversations

Informal conversations are invaluable for understanding the problem in mathematics instruction. Ask teachers, support staff, parents—and yes, students—questions about what they believe to be true about the mathematics program. Focus your attention on things that are under a school's control. Yes, we might hope that more parents will be involved in their children's educations, and that they will help their children with their math at home, but the reality is that some parents can't or won't. We cannot easily change that.

Ask questions such as these:

What does your school do well?
"We have good relationships with parents."
"We value students' native languages."
"We are good at assessing students and adjusting instruction."
"We really try to prepare students for the twenty-first century."

Consider whether these things match the end that you have in mind, and whether they directly affect student achievement.

Where can your school improve? Where does it fall short?
"Our teaching is inconsistent across the grades. Students are learning the teachers, not the mathematics."
"Our intermediate students have a lot of trouble with fractions."
"The students still don't know their multiplication tables."
"Teachers don't teach math every day. On half days math gets left out."
"My teacher doesn't respect us. So the kids give her a hard time."

Investigate the approaches that the school has already used to try to solve these problems. Look for different approaches. Make sure that teachers teach mathematics for at least a full hour each day, and that homework and review do not take the place of instructional time.

Where does success in mathematics come from?
"You just have to be smart."
"Mike is lucky—he's good in math."
"If you work hard, you'll be successful."

Students may attribute success to luck, and many adults in the United States believe that success in mathematics is inherited or genetic. On a conscious level students—and teachers—must understand that they control their own success.

What kind of instruction leads to success in math?
"You have to model a lot: I do, we do, you do is the key."
"Make sure that the students do two pages of math problems and homework each day."

"Don't spoon-feed the students. Give them problems and allow them to struggle and work together."

Less is more in mathematics classes; have students think deeply about fewer problems. And make sure that problem solving is the major approach to instruction. Guided practice with gradual release of responsibility to the learner is a tool, but this should be balanced with letting the students think and reason for themselves.

What does the pathway currently look like as a student moves from grade to grade? Do teachers teach in consistent ways? Do students' experiences build in a consistent way over the years?
"We all have different strengths in teaching. It's okay to teach in different ways."
"I like to teach fractions through cooking."
"Worksheets and practice are the only way kids learn."
"I hope I don't have Mr. Nelson in fourth grade. He gives hours of homework."

High-poverty students are less likely to come from academic homes. They are less likely to have had parents who explicitly engaged them in mathematical conversations and experiences. Students of poverty, and students who struggle in mathematics, depend on schoolwide consistency.

What do teachers, coaches, principals, students, and parents expect as end-of-the-year outcomes for their grade? What skills and concepts do they believe are most important for their grade level?
"In third grade you can only expect students to understand the concept of multiplication."
"My brother had to learn his timeses to 12 when he was in third grade."
"When I went to school, I only had to learn the traditional algorithm for multiplication—none of these confusing strategies. What was good enough for me is good enough for my kids."

Who are our experts at school? Which teacher has particularly strong knowledge of mathematics and how students learn mathematics? Who has especially sound teaching practices? Who among our leaders is more likely to influence and motivate others? Who is highly intentional and perseveres in the face of challenges?
"I know that Mrs. Fernandez won't give up on me."
"Ms. Parks really understands algebra."
"The other teachers really respect Mr. William's opinion."
"The kids really listen to Ms. Janson . . . and they listen to each other in her class."

Understanding the human resources at your school will help you leverage your system to change as efficiently as possible.

At all of the schools that we support, we gather a variety of kinds of data, not just data that is easy to quantify. Yes, we examine standardized test scores, and this information is a piece of the puzzle, but it is rarely specific enough to guide instruction. Yes, a student may receive a low score in fractions, but a teacher still must identify *why* that happened. Did that student just guess? Did he or she understand but make a computational error? Did he or she interpret the 2 and 3 in $\frac{2}{3}$ as whole numbers instead of a relationship?

Informal conversations with educators, students, and parents are extremely revealing. Discussions about student work help teachers, coaches, and principals understand the problem. We first examine student work from the most successful students. We frequently find that even the students who are seen as "excelling" are often not reaching their potential. Examining student work from typical and struggling students often reveals needs for differentiation. Student work of all kinds tells us how schools need to adjust their sails. When we consistently see a variety of strategies in student work (as in Figure 2.2), when we frequently notice that students are writing with academic vocabulary, when students nearly always include clear diagrams of their thinking and specific examples, we know that we are making significant progress.

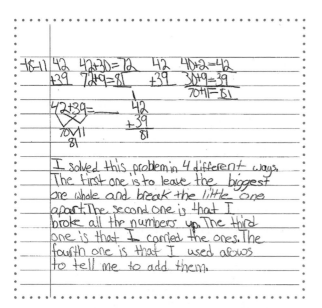

Figure 2.2 Rosamaria solved this problem in multiple ways.

Data from Lesson Observations

We gather data not only about the students, but also about ourselves as educators. If we observe students being passive during our lessons, we ask, "How often are we explicitly engaging them?" It helps when teachers, coaches, and principals observe each other's lessons, sometimes tallying the use of engagement strategies or level of questioning.

When we listen to students' math talk and hear imprecise, vague language, we ask, "How often do adults use mathematical terminology during lessons? And how often do we require this of students?" During coteaching lessons both coaches and teachers take notes on how they encourage explicit mathematics vocabulary, and share their findings with each other.

Data from Systemic Analysis Tools

The 4-Dimensional Analysis Tool (Figure 2.3) is an example of a tool that helps educators at a school site recognize their strengths and shape goals.

It analyzes the following:

° Content knowledge—understanding of mathematics and how concepts connect and build over time, and how skills support learning

° Instructional knowledge—understanding and use of best instructional practices and assessment strategies

° Management—the ability to motivate students, organize for instruction, and track student learning

° Leadership—interpersonal skills and dispositions that allow an educator to work well with others and positively influence the school culture

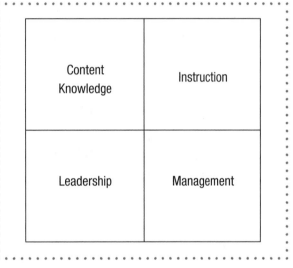

Figure 2.3 4-Dimensional Analysis Tool

It is important for principals, coaches, and teachers to reflect on their own skills in terms of these four attributes. Where are their strengths? Where is there a possibility for growth? This self-reflection, whether done privately or in small groups, can release incredible potential:

"I really like my units on probability. I could share them with my team."

"My management skills are strong. The new teacher might appreciate some pointers."

"I've never thought of myself as a leader. But people do listen when I talk at staff meetings. Maybe I could make more of a difference here."

Negative information can also have positive results:

"I don't understand decimals very well. During lunch I'll ask Ms. Jackson to explain how she approaches them."

"Positively influence others . . . ? Maybe I've been too negative lately."

Analysis of these attributes can help those who are most responsible for school change—often the principal and a leadership team—understand the players within any given school. Decisions such as grade-level assignments for teachers, prioritization of coaching time, and invitations to professional development can be based on thoughtful reflection about this data.

Data from Formative Assessments

Formative assessment is the tool that best adjusts and trims the sails of mathematics improvement from month to month, week to week, and day to day. Pre- and post-unit assessments observations, "quick-writes," student work (see Figure 2.4), and "closing problems" are examples of formative assessments that help both teachers and students understand the growth that they've made, and motivate everyone to continue their hard work. Formative assessments, more than any others, provide teachers, coaches, and principals with the diagnostic information that ultimately helps educators determine how to adjust lessons and units to maximize outcomes for students.

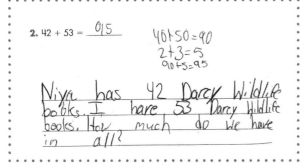

Figure 2.4 Unit assessment: Jackie's work demonstrates that she can create a story that matches the problem and that she can solve the problem using her knowledge of place value.

Identify "Next Steps," Take Action, and Evaluate

As we step forward at any school, we have to question whether our decisions in fact made a difference for students. Although it may sound easy, this can be the most difficult step of all. Hypotheses are usually based on beliefs. Beliefs are often near and dear to our hearts, and many of us find it difficult to challenge them.

"Giving the end-of-unit assessment to the students at the beginning of the unit will provide us with useful information." A sixth-grade teacher made this hypothesis. However, his teammate had many concerns about taking that step.

"The students will just feel like failures before they start," she said. "And they won't know any of the material, because we haven't taught it."

The team went ahead and tried preassessing to see what would actually happen. During a grade-level meeting they shared what they discovered.

"I was surprised at how well it turned out," the concerned teacher mused. "During the preassessment I reminded the kids that we hadn't learned the material yet. The kids were fine with just doing their best. And," she added, "after I reviewed their work, I realized they already knew about rotational symmetry and transformations. I realized that I could do a quick review and move on."

Schools who research their mathematics programs make numerous hypotheses and apply many remedies. It is important to remember that all children are capable of understanding mathematics and developing skills. "What will it take?" is the question.

Repeat the Cycle Again and Again

As educators better understand the problems that face them, their understanding naturally flows into new decisions, actions, adaptations, and eventually into changes in beliefs. Assumptions that once seemed to be true are proven untrue through school-based research. As it turns out:

- Most students *can* learn how to unravel complexity.
- Students remember better when they work with concrete materials.
- Accurate answers alone do not assure that students understand the content.

From time to time we encounter teachers who believe that students have to complete basic skills before they can solve problems. After observing a lesson where students first worked with partners to ask questions, gather data, create their own graphs, and share their data in a "math congress," another teacher decided to have her students do the same.

"If I hadn't seen that lesson, I wouldn't have considered letting my kids do that," the teacher explained. "And they really liked being in the driver's seat. They asked questions that I never would have thought about asking!"

The critical next move is to make these new ideas public, to make sure that others at the school benefit from discoveries that teams of teachers, the coach, and the principal make. New, effective ideas must be shared and celebrated . . . and encouraged throughout the building.

Problem solving is recursive. This means that as educators gather information, they find that they must understand the problem in its new aspects, over and over and over again. And they must continually gather data. With all the literature read, with all the professional development, with all the conversations, meetings, classes, and assessments, has the children's mathematics ability improved dramatically enough to justify the expense? Is the work paying off?

At any school where we support the change process, we have to clarify our problem statement many times: What does effective reasoning look like? When should we

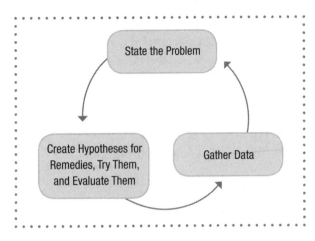

Figure 2.5 Understanding the problem is an ongoing process.

expect students to become efficient problem solvers? What does clear communication look like?

As we gather information, new subproblems emerge: Which knowledge and skills are important for each grade? How will we track student understanding? Problem solving is neither linear nor a recipe. We find that schools on the journey to new mathematics programs move between and among these phases (See Figure 2.5), adjusting and learning as the school culture changes.

"Problems Are Our Friends"

Michael Fullan (1993) said these profound words, which help us when we find ourselves in the midst of the anxiety that change inevitably brings. School change is never smooth sailing.

We believe that problems are opportunities in disguise:

°   *Are your second graders confused about fact families?*

The good news is that now you know that you need to take action. You need to back up to part/whole relationships and have them toss two-color counters and describe the whole amount that always stays the same and the changing parts that are yellow and red.

°   *Do you find that you have a group of teachers who are dragging their feet regarding the new math program?*

The good news is that now you know that you need to engage them in conversations about their concerns, which may help you understand the problem in a new way. During the discussion you might share how you understand the problem: that the students have limited number sense and passively memorize procedures. The teachers may have an entirely different understanding—but the conversation needs to happen.

Each problem that you face offers hidden possibilities. Keep open to the opportunities that accompany problems, and be flexible in your approach. Remember what a wise person once said: blessed are the flexible, for they shall not be bent out of shape!

Understanding the Problem

When schools sail toward improved mathematics programs, the question "What will it take?" must permeate informal conversations between teachers, the principal, the coach and other staff members, students, parents, and anyone with an interest and investment in the school. "What will it take?" should be the topic of schoolwide planning meetings as well as grade-level team discussions, budget meetings, and parent nights.

Identifying where you are—and where you want to be—is the best way to drive to a new vacation spot, to sail a boat back to shore, and to significantly change mathematics education at a school.

Take time to adjust your sails the right way—and keep on making adjustments. Understanding the problem is the most important step toward creating sustainable, predictable, and abundant places for students to learn mathematics.

The Principal's Perspective

I remember arriving at my new school, only to find that it had really dropped in its test scores. My first thought was, "What was I thinking in wanting to be a principal?" It was a little too late for that, of course.

I knew that the only way to get this system to another place was to understand the people there, to understand teachers' beliefs, values, content understanding, and priorities. Taking time to understand the problem required a daily commitment to talking methodically to teachers:

What are you working on today?
What do you expect the kids to learn in this lesson?

I spent a great deal of time talking to students:

What are you supposed to learn right now?
Why are you supposed to learn it?
Does the paper you are working on show what you're supposed to be learning?

At the end of the day, I would return to the classroom I observed, and we would look at the student work from that lesson (Figure 2.6).

I asked:

Did the kids learn what you wanted them to learn? Why do you think that happened or didn't happen?

What is so important in your grade that every student should leave with it by the end of the year?

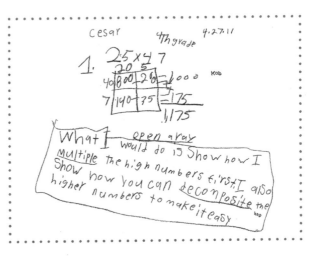

Figure 2.6 Student work

Answers to these questions told me that the educators at the school were working very hard and many good things were in place. Yet it became clear that we needed to make a cultural shift toward cohesive outcomes for students.

Our students needed smoother transitions as they progressed through the grades. Teachers had to understand that they are interdependent—that student learning in each grade depends on what happens in the previous grade. Teachers, the coach, and I as the principal all needed to become unified in understanding student learning pathways in math, and to work to create consistency within our math program.

My discussions with the teachers and the coach allowed me to better understand the strengths at my school, and led to discussions about how to capitalize on them. I consciously reflected on the characteristics of strong educators: content knowledge, instructional knowledge, management, and leadership. I did my best to prioritize what I observed in each person, as well as in myself, by quantifying each characteristic with the numbers 1, 2, 3, or 4.

This exercise opened my eyes to the abundant resources that were available in our system and that lie within any school. Then I worked with the teachers to capitalize on these strengths. For example, a teacher who was new to the school but had a high level of content knowledge shared about ratios during a staff meeting. I placed a less-organized teacher in a grade-level team with a well-organized colleague. A skilled first-year teacher had her students doing math at a high level, which created an example of possibility for a more complacent teacher in that same grade.

As I asked myself reflective questions and bounced them off other staff members, my working relationships with staff improved. As our defensive shielding dropped, trust and shared responsibility grew. Excitement, passion, and purpose were rekindled.

We had frank discussions about what "high expectations" meant. Turns out that high expectations were dependent not only on our content knowledge, but also on our awareness of our instructional practices. The more we learned, the more questions we had. This was to be a never-ending journey.

The Math Coach's Perspective

One of the more critical pieces of my work has been helping to shift the culture of our school. It's a daunting task: supporting the directions we were moving toward as a school while developing the trust of teachers. It's a really hard balance to strike.

My principal has made clear to the teachers that I'm not an evaluator. And they know that I don't do any official evaluations. But my job is very tricky; I walk a very fine line. My job is supporting school change, so I have to be alert to what works with students and what doesn't work—in a sense, evaluating lessons. When teaching isn't going well—for any reason—teachers can feel angry and hurt. It's natural, because they care a lot and have invested a lot of themselves in their kids.

That's why I try to maintain a friendly, light presence . . . and laugh at my mistakes. If I show that mistakes are just a natural part of the learning process, teachers feel freer to make their own inevitable mistakes as they hone their skills.

I work to build trust by honoring their confidences and being "one of them." I help them assess their children, do interventions, work to get their kids invested in math, whatever it takes. But whatever I do, I take advantage of opportunities to move our school forward. When Heidi draws a circle and divides it into "fourths" by drawing three parallel lines, I bring Ms. Nolan into a discussion about her misconception and how common it is. We wonder aloud about which other children have the same idea, and decide on a quick-write that will give us this information. When Alan mutters that he'll never be any good at math, I turn to Ms. Giffords and we think about how we can help him find a measure of success and recognize his growth.

So, although I'm not an evaluator, I'm responsible for helping the teachers and the principal grow. And I hope that they feel that same responsibility toward me, that we all are helping each other become more sensitive to students' needs, more adept at meeting those needs, and more knowledgeable about mathematics. We're all in this together. I am learning how to help teachers more effectively. When a teacher and I are talking about a challenge that we're having in the classroom, I try to keep our conversations specific so that we avoid falling into assumptions.

When teachers or the principal—or I—use the words *they always*, I know that we need to follow Bruce Wellman's advice in *Mentoring Matters: A Practical Guide to Learning-Focused Conversations* (2003). We shift the conversation toward more specificity, which gives us a better understanding of the problem. Exactly who is not paying attention? Is it everybody? When does that happen? Why might that be? Specifically describing the problem gives us clarity and helps us decide what to do. Yet sometimes I find us being too specific, focusing on individual children rather than the implications for our teaching in general. So I might shift the conversation to a more general level and ask the teacher which language development strategies were especially helpful to her English language learners.

The Teacher's Perspective

I know how important it is to understand the problem before identifying a solution. Goodness knows that our school has had lots of advice from outside people—especially when we didn't make our Adequate Yearly Progress goals. Some of the advice was from people who really didn't understand our needs.

Sometimes it seems like it's the principal who doesn't understand the problem and makes directives that take us in the wrong direction, away from what we really need to focus on. At one school where I worked, the principal had us write these very elaborate objectives, several per lesson, and they had to be written in a very specific way. I found that I was spending more time on objectives than on planning what I needed to do for my students! When you multiply all that time by each subject area, you end up expending most of your time and energy in writing objectives.

Although I think it's important to understand the objective that I'm teaching, I also need to be fully present to understanding the problems my students are having when they're doing math. My coach is really helpful here. She sees some things, and I see other things, and we get to the bottom of what's happening—together. And when we understand why one student is having problems, it helps us with other students as well.

For example, Margie was constantly having trouble comparing fractions. She kept interpreting the numerator and denominator as whole numbers. And she wasn't the only one. The circles she was drawing didn't seem to help at all (Figure 2.7).

When my coach and I met, I shared what I was seeing. I also told her how Margie is a very impulsive child. She likes to jump to answers in all subject areas, and I'm working with her on that. I have to be very specific with her. For example, I had to write out a set of procedures for her to do when she comes into the classroom every morning and tape it to her desk. Otherwise, I'd find her without a pencil and wanting to use the restroom right when we were ready to start writing workshop.

My coach and I kept that important information in mind when we looked at Margie's work. Since the circles made it hard for Margie to compare the size of the fractions, we decided that the bar model would be more effective for that—and that it would

Figure 2.7 Margie's fractions

help all the students. We decided to immerse the kids in an experience highlighting the need for the two bars to be an equivalent size. Then we planned an explicit, step-by-step, lesson with "I do [my modeling], we do [doing it with students], and you do [students working independently]" that would especially fit Margie's needs.

Chapter 3
The Stance of a Researcher

A man checks into a hotel for the first time ever, and goes up to his room.
A moment later he calls the front desk and cries into the phone,
"You've given me a room with no exit! How can I possibly leave?"
The manager responds, "Sir, that's ridiculous. Just look for the door!"
The man peers around the room. Then he answers, "I see a bathroom door
and a closet door. I tried both of them. There's another door that I haven't tried,
but it has a 'Do Not Disturb' sign on it."

Walk into almost any school, and pretty quickly you get a sense of what that school is all about. Quotes on the wall, student work in the hallway, as well as how adults and children speak to each other all paint a picture of what is valued in any school.

What is less clear to a visitor is how that value system came about. Was it the result of teachers following directives from an administrator? Or did the change come about through teacher research, where teachers discover what works best?

We believe that sustainable change happens when teachers are invited to remove the "Do Not Disturb" signs that protect their long-standing assumptions about "how we do school." Incredible potential is released when teachers are in the driver's seat, actively involved in making sense of how to teach mathematics in the most engaging, relevant, and meaningful way possible.

Some educators might think that how teachers develop habits of instruction and interaction are beside the point; simply getting teachers to leave old habits behind is sufficient, regardless of how they got there. An ad for tennis shoes insists we should "just do it," and many administrators agree. However, we know that having teachers just follow directives leads to low-level, inconsistent implementation, which is likely to disappear whenever the principal leaves the building for the moment or forever. Instead, we urge, "Just research!"

Teacher, Coach, and Principal as Researcher: Unpacking the Mysteries

"Do Not Disturb" signs are as varied as educators themselves. These signs continually mask hidden potential by blocking teacher learning and limiting possibilities for children. Research, for us, extends far beyond university or lab school settings, past professors or formal papers, and comes to rest directly in the hearts and minds of teachers. Certainly any day in the classroom bubbles over with surprises in student learning, inconsistencies that are ripe and ready for teacher reflection and investigation.

When confronted with a child who makes a mistake, a "Do Not Disturb" sign might make a teacher say that the child wasn't paying attention or cause a teacher to reteach the idea in the same way, using the "slower and louder" approach. In contrast, a teacher-researcher sees the error as an opportunity to discover more about how children learn mathematics and to develop more effective teaching responses (Figure 3.1). Teacher research requires teachers to move from spontaneous reaction, to reflection, and then action.

Figure 3.1 This second-grade teacher is researching which strategies best help her students count coins.

Take any moment in the classroom. Listen carefully to what children say and do as they work to solve a mathematics problem. A child's unexpected idea or action is a doorway into his or her own unique logic, and opens up potentially powerful ways for teachers to respond. Take the time to stop, look, and wonder about what is occurring before your eyes.

Kayla, a third grader, draws a 2-by-3 rectangular array by making disconnected squares (Figure 3.2). "I really think she's trying," says Ms. Blaylock. "What does Kayla not see? Is what she did typical?"

After watching her, Ms. Blaylock worries that Kayla won't be able to understand how arrays represent equal groups in multiplication, which is the focus of the current classroom work. Ms. Blaylock talks to her math coach, who shares with her an article about children's developing understandings about arrays. Ms. Blaylock discovers that many children who are just beginning to make sense of arrays draw pictures similar to Kayla's.

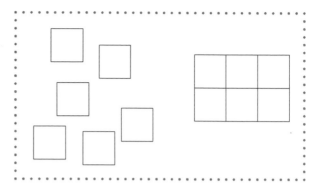

Figure 3.2 Kayla draws disconnected squares (left) instead of an organized 2-by-3 array (right).

"I'm guessing Kayla's not the only one in my class who doesn't see the arrangement as rows with equal groups in each row," Ms. Blaylock says. She realizes now that Kayla's perception is a normal step in the learning pathway. With this powerful discovery, Ms. Blaylock works to develop questions and create learning experiences to help Kayla confront an idea that will otherwise hinder her use of arrays in multiplication. And, more important, Ms. Blaylock generalizes from Kayla to all students, as she makes a note to be prepared for this same response when she teaches multiplication in subsequent years.

After reading, reflecting, and talking to other teachers, Ms. Blaylock comes up with two ideas to help Kayla. She invites Mia, a more experienced mathematics student, to work with Kayla to build a variety of arrays and talk about what they did first, second, and third, thereby focusing Kayla's attention on the equal rows and columns in each array. Ms. Blaylock also provides Kayla with partially drawn arrays, and encourages her to examine an array's structure by finding out how many squares should be in the entire array when it is completed (Figure 3.3).

After several of these experiences, Kayla successfully uses arrays to represent multiplication problems, and Ms. Blaylock is pleased that she has developed a repertoire of new, rich teaching tools. Ms. Blaylock shares her research during grade-level meeting time that week.

In another classroom, Mr. Suarez, a kindergarten teacher with a solid

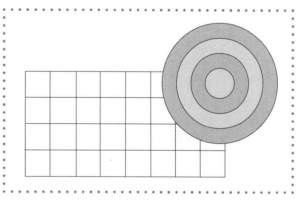

Figure 3.3 A rug covers part of a tiled floor. How many tiles are there?

Figure 3.4 Julio counts and says, "Here is 'three.'"

research perspective, asks Julio to count some pennies. "One, two, three," counts Julio, touching each penny once. Mr. Suarez smiles, pleased that Julio just demonstrated one-to-one correspondence. But he doesn't stop there; he asks Julio to "Show me three." (See Figure 3.4.)

Julio pushes the third penny toward him, and Mr. Suarez's eyebrows rise in surprise. "Why doesn't Julio show me all three pennies?" he wonders.

It occurs to Mr. Suarez that when Julio counts, he is naming each penny with a number word, similar to naming each penny "Carrie," "Richard," and "Scott." When Mr. Suarez asked Julio to show him "three," Julio showed him the third penny, demonstrating that he does not understand "cardinality"—that a number is a quantity, and that it includes all of the other elements, or numbers, within the set (Figure 3.5).

Mr. Suarez decides to have Julio confront the quantity of three by giving him the daily job of counting the children sitting at his table and retrieving that number of pen-

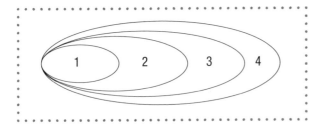

Figure 3.5 Four is a quantity that includes all of the other items that were counted.

cils for them. He also resolves to consistently ask less experienced children to count, and then to either ask them to show him that number or ask them, "So how many are there?" Mr. Suarez realizes that, without asking those questions, he might think that the children understand counting at a deeper level than they really do.

Teacher research often takes place informally; it is a habit of mind and a way of looking at learning within a classroom. But research can also take place formally with all the teachers at a school thinking and learning about a specific idea. At one school, the teachers all decided to focus on visual models for addition, determining which ones they thought were most effective in specific math topics. At another school, the teachers in one grade level worked hard on developing mathematical language, sharing their most effective strategies. The staff of still another school, which had a high population of Native American children, capitalized on the funds of knowledge in their community by exploring pattern units in their community's pottery designs.

Any school can be a research school, and any teacher can be a researcher. It all depends on how educators view themselves. Schools typically are full of doors that educators avoid opening. Imaginary "Do Not Disturb" signs in the form of assumptions often dangle their warnings, stopping educators from questioning what is most near and dear to their hearts. But to us, research schools are schools where well-informed educators are free to open any door, and to question everything that they do.

"Just Do It" Mathematics Programs

In the same way that there are a great deal of "Just Do It" methods of school improvement, there are many examples of "Just Do It" mathematics programs. If you are like most people, the common joke "Yours is not to reason why, just invert and multiply" makes you laugh somewhat uncomfortably because it reminds you of how you learned to divide fractions: by being told to memorize a procedure. For the problem $\frac{1}{2} \div \frac{1}{4}$ you would have been instructed to invert the $\frac{1}{4}$ to make the problem $\frac{1}{2} \times \frac{4}{1}$. Multiplying across the numerators and denominators (never mind why that works in multiplication but not in addition!), you get the answer $\frac{4}{2}$ or 2. Reasoning why was not part of the equation.

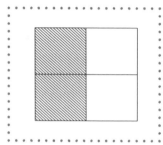

Figure 3.6 There are two fourths in half a brownie.

However, it is easy to reason through that question by asking, "How many fourths are in a half?" You might illustrate the question by creating a diagram of a whole square, and then shading in one half of it (Figure 3.6). How many fourths are inside that half? It's easy to see that there are two of them.

When we first took on our positions as principal and math coach at Pueblo Gardens Elementary School, we were clear that there was no "math gene" that imparts mathematical understanding to some children but not to others, and that these high-poverty children could be highly successful in mathematics. To do this, we were convinced that we wanted to implement a mathematics program that we had used at other schools, one that required children to make sense of mathematics. Teachers at Pueblo Gardens Elementary were acquainted with this program, since these materials had been available at the school for a few years as a supplement to a more traditional mathematics program. Some teachers had used the program that we liked intermittently, but others had chosen not to use it at all. To create a true culture of research, we knew this program had to become a focus of our schoolwide research.

So we put our preferred mathematics program itself under the lens of inquiry. Yes, we had a clear picture of the result we wanted from our school's mathematics program: children had to think, reason, problem solve, and communicate their ideas with mathematical language. But at the same time, we held fast to the idea that, if our assumptions didn't create real results for children, if in the final analysis children didn't become competent mathematicians and show what they knew on state tests, we would have to rethink even the program that we liked. At Pueblo Gardens, everything had to be on the table, open for discussion.

At that time, our research stance about curriculum was contrary to the beliefs that were part of our state's school improvement directives and many national movements to increase student achievement. The mantra that pervaded just about every professional development session that we were required to attend was "fidelity to the core." Rigid adherence to a given sequence of lessons, a "one-size-fits-all" approach even to the lessons themselves, was the order of the day.

But how could we, as principal and math coach, aspire to have students who were good problem solvers without encouraging teachers to be good problem solvers as well? Our goals for students inevitably had to influence our goals for teachers. We could not ask students to think and reason, and then require teachers to blindly march through a curriculum. And we could not chant "absolute fidelity to the core" while asking students to make sense of mathematics.

As with all of our schools, we began our work at Pueblo Gardens Elementary School by providing our teachers with the best professional development opportunities that we could find or create. And we worked with them to implement the mathematics program at a high level. Then in the spirit of high-quality research, we asked teachers to use the new mathematics materials in their entirety to understand how they functioned, in order to make sound judgments about them. In the end we intended to carefully examine the student outcomes and put that mathematics program itself to the test; it would have to prove itself in meeting our goals. Depending on the outcome, we would maintain what worked, and modify or eliminate what didn't work.

In the final analysis, the teachers agreed that although the program was highly successful in how it developed mathematical concepts, it fell somewhat short in providing students chances to practice skills to fluency. Teachers found a variety of ways to shore up that part of the program, and even today they continually search for ways to raise the bar for student learning. In every school where we work, we find that the mathematics program has to be adjusted in some way to maintain a balance that is appropriate for the students at the school.

Leveling the Playing Field: Everyone Is a Researcher

We believe that the most effective research schools are the result of leveling the playing field between teachers and principals. When principals research their own teaching of mathematics, they send a clear signal to their staffs: "I am highly committed to changing how mathematics is taught. I am so committed that I'm making my work in classrooms a priority." In doing this, a principal moves from "selling" the change process to living the change process. It signals the high status that research has in this educational community, and shows that mathematical change is so vital for the success of students that the principal is allocating that most precious, limited commodity—time.

Rather than simply talking about instructional strategies and telling teachers to make changes, the principal becomes fully engaged in understanding for him- or herself how children learn mathematical ideas, why specific ideas are fragile for children, and how to best support children down the pathway to new understandings. Only principals who research mathematics teaching can engage teachers in authentic discussions about their own understanding of connections between mathematics concepts, of why students make specific errors, or about developing their own and students' mathematical vocabulary.

Principals and teachers become colleagues in making sense of conceptual development and how to balance it with skill fluency, and in so doing, a schoolwide value system is created. It is this schoolwide culture of mathematics that allows teachers to affect the knowledge of other teachers; this culture creates a sustainable system that grows from within.

Mr. Henderson, principal of a rural, low-income school, immediately embraced this idea. "It makes sense to me, and I'll do anything to make our mathematics program effective," he said. That day he met with a fourth-grade teacher, and they planned and then cotaught a lesson on geometry. Although the classroom teacher took the lead in the lesson, Mr. Henderson participated by talking with the students while they worked on the problem (Figure 3.7), and he began the class discussion about the strategies that they used. Later he told the teachers, "I had no idea that when I drew an angle and talked about measuring it, the kids thought I meant how long the ray was! I understand more than ever the importance of having students explain their thinking. If I had not done that, I would have never known that they weren't even in the same ballpark that I was."

When Mr. Henderson shared his classroom experience, the teachers understood at a gut level that he was

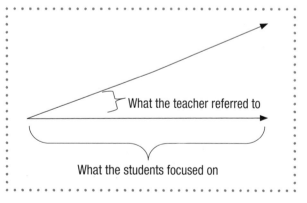

Figure 3.7 Mr. Henderson discussed angles, referring to the spread between rays. Instead students looked at how long the rays were.

"one of them." He was doing the same work in the classroom that the teachers did, and they respected his opinions more than ever. Mr. Henderson's example from his own teaching reminded the teachers, too, that it was critical to have their own students explain their thinking as often as possible.

This profoundly shifts the traditional roles of principals and teachers:

Traditional Roles

Principal as leader and evaluator: Observes lessons using an observation form based on best practices.

Instructional coach as "fixer": Observes lessons and gives feedback on areas of weakness.

Teacher as practitioner: Plans lessons, teaches lessons, and modifies lessons based on principal's feedback.

New Roles

Principal as practitioner: Periodically plans lessons, coteaches lessons, modifies his or her own practices, shares new learning with others, and leads professional development based on research.

Coach as leader: Plans lessons, teaches and coteaches lessons, modifies own practices based on classroom research, shares new learning with others, and leads professional development based on research.

Teacher as leader: Plans lessons, teaches and coteaches lessons, modifies his or her own practices, shares new learning with others, and leads professional development based on research.

The power of research lies in the fact that anyone at the school can be the catalyst for any other person's professional growth. Hierarchies diminish and are replaced by limitless potential. A coach can affect a principal's growth. A teacher can affect a coach's professional growth. Children can affect the thinking and growth of a teacher. Anyone in the system now has the potential to help anyone else grow and learn. Abundance, not scarcity, paints a picture of possibility.

No Blame

A culture of research requires belief in "no blame." Research in the real world has as many negative outcomes as positive ones. And that negative information is very informative;

learning what doesn't work is often an important step in discovering what does work. Thomas Edison finally created a successful light system to replace candles and gaslight in 1878 after thousands of failed attempts. As he made yet another incandescent bulb that failed, he commented, "I am not discouraged, because every wrong attempt discarded is another step forward."

Few mathematics lessons are shining examples of perfection, although we always aspire for high-quality instruction. Perhaps perfection is less a goal than is teachers becoming intensely aware of their teaching decisions, how students respond, and consistently incorporating more and better instructional patterns that move children forward.

In learning mathematics, children, too, make mistakes. The mathematical environment that we create for students must frame mistakes not as unfortunate errors to be quickly swept away, but instead as opportunities to learn something new.

Ms. Granillo, a second-grade teacher, asks her students to solve the following word problem:

> I want to celebrate that our class learned their doubles addition facts. So I want to bring 2 new pencils to give each student to keep. There are 19 students in our class. How many pencils do I need to bring?

After she makes certain that the children understand the problem, they take blank papers and move to their tables. A few children work together, but many prefer to work independently. Ms. Granillo notices that only one child uses cubes, whereas all the others prefer to illustrate the problem on paper. She wonders why that is the case, since she had believed that cubes are more concrete and would be easier for children to use. Ms. Granillo reminds herself to bring that up during grade-level teacher meetings. She then moves from table to table, observing children at work and engaging them in discussions about what they are doing.

Ms. Granillo watches Justine draw 19 circles to represent student faces, and then draw 2 lines for pencils above each face (Figure 3.8). Next Justine counts the circles and writes "*19 pencils I conted them.*"

Figure 3.8 Justine made circles for the students and 2 lines for the pencils that each student needed. Then she counted the circles, and decided that the teacher needs to get 19 pencils.

Ms. Granillo understands that this problem is deceptively difficult for children of this age. It involves multiplicative thinking, which many young children struggle with: one number describes how many children there are, and the other tells how many pencils each child has. Ms. Granillo notices that other children in the class are confused as well: do they count the children or the pencils? She decides to highlight this important question in the class discussion. Errors are neither bad nor a source of embarrassment, even for older students. Errors are merely opportunities to learn.

Avoiding the Name Trap

A "Do Not Disturb" sign that prevents educators from questioning their work is the "Name Trap." Principals, coaches, and teachers occasionally adopt a pedagogical technique, a way to organize a school, or a program of instruction, and apply it indiscriminately across the board. Although these ideas are often well conceived and beneficial, they can also take on a life of their own, sometimes to the detriment of the school.

In the 1970s a Name Trap might have been "We are an open classroom school." During that decade, open schools—with few interior walls and larger groups of students taught by several teachers—became popular in some areas. As a result, noise and disruption often became problems. Since then, many schools that were built with permanent "open classrooms" have been remodeled with permanently closed classroom walls. The potential benefits of that approach have been lost. Instead, a more beneficial approach to those interested in open schools might have been to ask questions:

° What are the potential benefits of open classrooms? How might they leverage our system to help us reach our long-term goals?
° What are some possible negative outcomes that we don't anticipate? Are they minor or will they have a significant negative effect on our long-term goals?
° Are there specific schools or populations, or even subject areas, where this arrangement makes particular sense?
° Might there be parts of a school campus that should be structured openly?
° Would a flexible structure that can be open or closed in specific instances better meet our overall needs?

Some current Name Traps appear with words such as these: "We believe in play," "We do TIMSS [Third International Mathematics and Science Study] math," "We are an accelerated learning school," "We are a back-to-basics school," or "We are a direct instruction school."

You can add to this list without much difficulty. Many Name Traps contain ideas that are important and provide valuable strategies for schools. However, indiscriminate application of any idea is nearly always a problem and is the root of the many educational bandwagons that our profession is often guilty of creating. Committing ourselves to researching was the best way we knew to avoid the Name Trap, and to make ourselves accountable to real outcomes for children.

The Stance of a Researcher

Today's profound shifts in technology and globalization have resulted in significantly higher expectations for students in mathematics. We know that students and teachers can rise to this challenge—we continually live this transformation—but we are convinced that a school with a culture of research is key.

Unlike the man in the hotel room who was inclined to follow the directive on the "Do Not Disturb" sign, teachers must be encouraged to open doors, to discover the possibilities that lie dormant within themselves and children, and to set them free.

The Principal's Perspective

I remember early on confronting a Name Trap and realizing its power over even highly accomplished teachers. At one of my schools, I found that our early childhood staff was firmly divided into those who "believed in play" and those who wanted some academic instruction in kindergarten. Rather than discussing the merits of each position and carving out a place that would make sense for our particular children, the discussion had deteriorated into win-lose disagreements. I finally had to intervene.

"I don't want to hear about philosophies," I told the group. "We've got to look at outcomes for kids."

The discussion certainly wasn't easy. We examined the knowledge and skills that these children bring with them the first day of school. We researched the reading and math outcomes that children had from grade to grade. We found that the majority of children did not enter school with the readiness skills that might be expected in many schools. And our outcomes clearly were poor—too many children left our elementary school for middle school without the tools to be successful.

It became clear that somehow we needed to increase our academic expectations and the academic learning time in kindergarten. At the same time we were determined to make academic learning engaging to young children. We acknowledged the learning, choices, and fun that high-quality play experiences provided for young children, so we resolved to significantly increase our reading and math expectations, and the time that children spent in those areas. But we also put additional resources into our music program, staffing it with one of our most capable early childhood teachers to capitalize on the playful learning opportunities that were so much a part of music.

Confronting the Name Trap and replacing it with research took time and energy. But in the end teachers professionally confronted their assumptions and created a solution that they thought would best meet the needs of their particular students.

Keeping my focus on research helps me in many other ways. I easily find myself reacting to all the urgent situations that seem to make their way to my door. At any given moment I'm bombarded by discipline problems, personnel issues, district requirements, lockdowns . . . you name it. I have to consciously stop and get myself off this all-consuming roller coaster. Everything simply is not a crisis. I have to move myself from reaction to reflection. Rather than constantly reacting by hitting the proverbial ping-pong ball back and forth, I instead stop the game. I pick up that ball; I examine it. For a moment, at least, I remove myself from the action.

Taking on the stance of a researcher calls me to wonder why people do what they do and to work to understand how others are thinking. Research reminds me about the importance of puzzling over how things can be better. I remind myself that abundance lives in my school, in the classrooms, in my community. Your thoughts are what you become. I remind myself to let go of my ego and to appreciate being in the company of children and teachers who learn from each other and are competent together.

The Math Coach's Perspective

Maintaining the stance of a researcher is critical to how I see my job. I have to remind the teachers that although I am fortunate to have focused on and learned a lot about mathematics, I am still learning alongside them. This frees the teachers to ask questions themselves, perhaps even reveal their own fragile understanding of mathematics. At my school we are the people with the questions as much as the answers. And the more we know, the more we realize that there is more to learn!

One day I had finished coteaching a math lesson with a second-grade teacher. During this lesson students solved a series of subtraction problems. Many of the children used the number line to solve the problems, but some of them counted forward from the smaller number. This bothered the teacher.

"We have to show the kids how to go to the left on the number line, because they are subtracting," she said.

"Hmm," I answered. "Do you have to go to the left for subtraction?"

The teacher paused to think. She took out the student work where the kids had counted forward. "They got the same answer," she said. "But to subtract, you have to take away. That means that you have to move backward."

Her statement told me that I needed to help her understand that there are different kinds of subtraction, so I moved from a collaborative coaching stance to a consultation stance, from which I would share some information that she needed to know. I opened her teacher guide to the section on subtraction, which said that subtraction can be represented in two kinds of situations: by removal or as a difference.

Here is an example of a removal story:

There were 41 apples in a tree. Then the wind blew 16 apples off. How many apples were still in the tree?

I used the same numbers and turned them into a difference story:

During a concert 41 children were wearing red shirts and 16 children were wearing yellow shirts. How many more children wore red shirts than yellow shirts?

I suggested that we use a number line to solve the first problem. The teacher worked backward on the open number line, showing how she took away 10, then 1, and then 5. She drew the diagram in Figure 3.9, and circled the answer: 25.

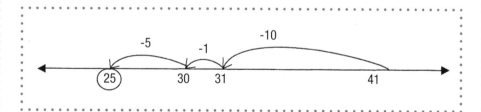

Figure 3.9 The teacher subtracted by counting back on an open number line.

Then we turned to the second problem. The teacher quickly discovered that for her it made more sense to count forward from 16 to solve the problem. She drew the diagram in Figure 3.10, and again circled the answer: 25.

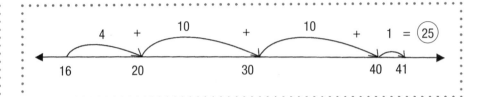

Figure 3.10 This time the teacher subtracted by adding up on an open number line.

"The answer is the same," the teacher said. "I guess you can subtract going either way on the number line."

I agreed, and added, "Interestingly enough, it seems to me that most children find it easier to add when solving subtraction problems. See what you think about that when your students are working. But when the problem is presented in a removal context, children often do what you had talked about: they move left on the number line and take away parts."

"That's interesting," the teacher said as she compared the two number lines. "The answer is on the line itself when you move backward, and it is in the total number of jumps when you count forward. I didn't know that. I wonder whether that will be confusing to the children."

"Let's find out," I suggested, and we created a series of difference problems for the children and planned the lesson for the next day.

The Teacher's Perspective

I find myself continually raising the bar with my students. Before they solve a problem, I usually have in my mind what I think they can do. If they meet my expectations, I wonder where else I can push them. And I have to say, sometimes they're as amazed as I am at their incredible work.

For example, today we had a lesson on characteristics of angle pairs. The text had students use protractors to measure opposite or "vertical" angles where two lines intersect, and had them use this information to "prove" that vertical angles measure the same and therefore are congruent (see Figure 3.11). The text walked them through the answer by measuring rather than letting the students reason to solve the problem for themselves.

I really don't think that simply measuring a number of sets of vertical angles constitutes a proof. To me that's not a proof, since measurement is never exact and the numbers they will come up with often won't add up to 180 degrees.

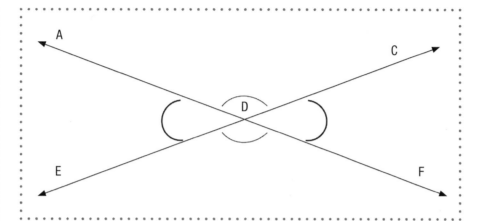

Figure 3.11

I think I'm going to open up this problem from the beginning, to see whether my students can figure this out for themselves. I don't think that they'll need to measure at all! All the information they need is in the diagram. They know that angle ADC and angle CDF equal 180 degrees, because they create a straight angle. And angles CDF and FDE also equal 180 degrees. So angles ADC and FDE must be equal because they share the same supplementary angle.

I think I'll also con-
nect two straws in the
middle with a pushpin
to demonstrate how the
angles relate. When we
rotate the perpendicular
"lines" around the pin,
the students can explore
how vertical and supple-
mentary angles change.
I think that my students
are capable of making
sense of this. I think that
how the textbook struc-
tures this particular task
underestimates the kids.

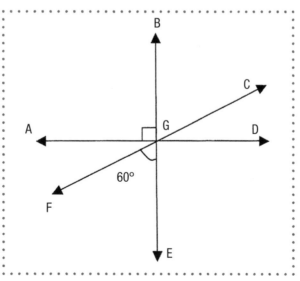

Figure 3.12 Given this diagram with two labeled angles, students can identify each of the other angles.

Then I read another problem in today's lesson. The students are asked to use the diagram in Figure 3.12 and identify all the angles that are not given.

I examined the anchor papers that the lesson provided for a high-quality, level 4 answer, and I have to say that I know my students can do much better work. To begin with, the rubric doesn't require the students to use mathematical vocabulary, but I expect my students to always use words such as *congruent* and *vertical angles* in their written explanations.

I also know that my students can solve this problem in more than one way. The text requires just one way—a method that is based on the fact that vertical angles are congruent. My students are used to the expectation that they will solve problems in more than one way. I wondered what other strategies they might use, in addition to vertical angles. So I'm definitely going to adjust the lesson. I know that my students can exceed the standard, but they won't if I don't aim high.

Chapter 4
The 80/20 Rule

If you can organize your kitchen, you can organize your life.

—Louis Parrish

Most of us know how to organize kitchens. Marco strategically places his grandmother's spatula, which he uses almost daily, in the drawer next to the stove. He keeps his lemon squeezer—which he needs only when he makes lemon bars—in the out-of-the-way drawer that sticks, along with a jumble of other things of limited use.

Principals, coaches, and teachers also have an 80 percent drawer and a 20 percent drawer where they allot time for things that they see as more important and less important. Examine what's inside your 80 percent drawer and 20 percent drawer—you quickly get a picture of your priorities. Ultimately what is most important gets done, and what is less important gets relegated to tomorrow's to-do list.

What if principals, coaches, and teachers maintained 80 percent of their attention on the things that matter most, things that are likely to move the system forward? What if they spent only 20 percent of their time on the have-tos and the things that are less likely to have a long-term positive effect on their school? How much more forward momentum might occur at a school? And how much faster might the school culture shift?

As Stephen Covey (2004) says, "The key is not to prioritize what's on your schedule, but to schedule your priorities." The 80/20 Rule provides a similar organizational structure to support decision making in schools. The 80/20 Rule guides educators in determining how to use the very limited and precious resources of time, energy, and money to increase positive outcomes for students.

Cost-Benefit Analysis

School budgets tighten up each year, and requirements for record-keeping devour more and more time. How conscious are principals, coaches, and teachers of the cost of each decision that they make about time, money, and energy? Spending resources in one place inevitably requires giving up something else.

If a teacher has to spend time creating lessons day after day, he may not have time to assess student learning. Ask: How might teachers share resources?

If a math coach spends time organizing a schoolwide math competition, she may be less prepared the next day to help a teacher respond to a child who doesn't understand multiplication. Ask: Should the math coach focus on classroom instruction instead?

If a principal spends time disciplining the daily line of students sent to the office, she may not be engaged in productive conversations with teachers. Ask: Can the teachers buddy up for student "time-out"? Does the school have a solid discipline program? Can the principal take a frustrated student with him to a classroom lesson and let the student cool off while the principal participates in the lesson?

Certainly, creating lessons, organizing math competitions, and managing students can be beneficial and important. However, it is imperative for principals, coaches, and teachers to keep in mind what they are giving up, and consider whether the trade-off is worth the cost. Maintaining focus on the broader vision and mission is critical, to keep sight of what is most important. While caught up in the whirlwind of issues and demands, educators must take a moment to examine the tasks, each of which bears the label "Must Do Now," to determine if it really is a priority.

What economists call "cost-benefit analysis" is a useful strategy for successful school change. This strategy, when internalized by all school personnel, becomes a way of being and part of the school culture. When anyone—a teacher, coach, or principal—makes a choice about what to do during instructional time, planning time, needs assessments, or budget meetings, the cost-to-benefit question must remain front and center.

Schools are not businesses. Children's knowledge is the goal rather than monetary profit, so *cost* and *benefit* must be defined in nonmonetary terms. The cost is what educators give up in order to do something. The benefit is the long-term or short-term payoff in relation to the school's primary goal—in this instance, improvement of student understanding and achievement in mathematics.

Layering on Activities

Conflicting needs that fill most schools with tension defy the imagination of most nonprofessionals. In the midst of this turbulence, solutions, activities, and programs are layered one on top of another, until the proverbial camel becomes loaded to a backbreaking point.

Teachers teach lessons in all content areas; prepare parent workshops, hallway bulletin boards, and homework programs; assess students; teach interventions; collect money for Picture Day; keep Barbara from bullying Joni; and maintain highly detailed lesson plans complete with language and content objectives for each content area.

Coaches' time overflows with substituting in classrooms and for the principal, intervening with student behavior, analyzing standardized test data, running programs for progress monitoring, coordinating intervention programs, teaching demonstration lessons, facilitating professional development study groups, and coaching sessions, often while maintaining meticulous records about teacher support.

Principals are asked to be instructional leaders but at the end of the day might realize that they did not set foot within a classroom because of the leaky roof, two angry parents, district reports, teacher conflicts, a missing substitute, a playground fight, program needs assessments, and the frustrated, out-of-control kindergartner who wailed for forty-five minutes.

We get it. Educators' lives are filled to overflowing with decisions and demands. However, it is imperative to separate the "imperative" from "important," and to think creatively about how to maintain classroom instruction at the forefront, where it belongs.

It is critical for coaches and principals to schedule time *in* classrooms, working alongside teachers, keeping their eyes on the prize of high-quality classroom instruction. Fill up your calendars first with what will most likely move your culture forward. When planning programs, consciously consider the cost of a decision, what must be given up in return, and whether that cost is worth paying.

The 80/20 Rule
1. Always "Keep the end in mind."
2. Do a cost-benefit analysis for decisions: before committing your time, energy, and money, consider your perceived benefits and your costs—what you *won't* be able to do if you decide to take that action.
3. Identify whether the benefits are likely to have a direct payoff for your goals and whether it is worth giving up the cost.
4. Work toward making decisions that allow you to spend 80 percent of your time, energy, and money on the things that matter most, and 20 percent on things that have less payoff.

An Example of High Cost, Low Benefit

A high-poverty school had a great principal, capable teachers, a good school culture . . . and consistently low test scores in math.

"We really believe that these kids can be good mathematicians, and we're doing everything that we're supposed to do," the principal said, his voice cracking in frustration.

When he was asked about the schoolwide focus, he recited this list:

○ A new mathematics program
○ A new writing program
○ A new grant for an after-school program for children
○ Evening astronomy events for families
○ On-site university classes for teachers to learn more math and science
○ Math and parenting classes for parents
○ Teacher home visits to connect content to students' lives

"It's a lot," the principal admitted. "Maybe too much. But they're all good things."

Clearly he, his teachers, and the math coach had a great deal on their plates. Using the 80/20 Rule, the principal recounted what it took for the teachers to do the last item—connecting instruction to students' home lives:

○ Scheduling and making home visits
○ Calling parents to plan and schedule parent presentations to classrooms about how they use mathematics
○ Sending home individual letters as reminders
○ Gathering necessary materials and making alternative plans in the event that a parent didn't come after all
○ Using grade-level planning time to discuss how to connect the curriculum to what the parents had shared

What was the benefit?

"We want parents to feel empowered about their understanding of content and their ability to help their children at school," the principal explained. "And students will feel pride in their families, and will understand that math and science are tools that will help them in life."

These are all laudable goals, many of which may be reached. But these questions must be asked: What is the *likelihood* that this time will translate into real changes in students' perceptions? And more important, will there be *direct* payoff in terms of the students' knowledge and skills, and their abilities to succeed in school mathematics?

"I'm not sure," the principal concluded reluctantly.

What was the overall cost? The principal outlined the following:

- ° Since teachers made home visits, they lost planning time for seven days, so their mathematics lessons were less effective.
- ° Since parent presentations took place during mathematics instructional time, teachers eliminated five lessons that they had planned.
- ° The cohesive unit of instruction was interrupted and became more fragmented.
- ° During grade-level professional development time, teachers scheduled parent presentations rather than analyzing end-of-unit assessments and organizing interventions.

After reviewing this list, the principal admitted, "I don't usually think about our choices in terms of what we are giving up. When I think about the cost, it's much more than I had imagined. And the benefit is less predictable than I had realized. Perhaps right now the teachers should spend time on their own professional development, their math instruction, and assessing student understanding and skills. I can guarantee that will pay off for the students.

"Although home visits and connecting to students' lives is important," the principal continued, "it will benefit the children only if instruction is solid to begin with."

Choices are hard. But it is necessary for schools to make choices consciously. Saying "yes" to one thing requires you to say "no" or perhaps "not yet" to something else.

At this school, the principal next considered the goals that he had hoped the home visits and parent presentations would achieve:

- ° Children's voices and cultures would be heard in the classroom, and their different gifts would contribute to school learning.
- ° Students' different ideas and perspectives would be respected.
- ° Students would be more likely to make sense of math that comes from their homes than "school math."

Then the principal considered how their mathematics program could meet some of these same goals:

- ° Students are encouraged to think for themselves as they solve problems, using models and strategies that make sense to them.
- ° Different solutions are respected and discussed, and students try out strategies that their peers present.
- ° Problems in the math program are often presented through real-life contexts and engaging problems.

"I can see that right now we need to work on our goals through our mathematics curriculum," the principal determined. "Right now we all need to keep our focus on instruction and evidence of student learning. I can *count* on the children benefiting from that. Perhaps next year, when the teachers' math instruction is more solid, we might spend time in other ways. But not now."

Examples of Low Cost, High Benefit

In our roles as coach and principal at Pueblo Gardens Elementary School, we had innumerable conversations over the years about the 80/20 Rule and learned to use it to guide our decisions. Over time the school's culture shifted markedly to a focus on student learning. Not only did test scores in several classrooms immediately rise, but, most important, students and teachers learned to love math.

We worked to focus our time and energy on the mathematics and literacy programs that the staff identified as fundamental to improving the chances for future success for these low-income students—children who arrived at Pueblo Gardens Elementary School with the same high potential that all children have. Maintaining focus was not easy, and we didn't do it perfectly. And, as coach and principal, we certainly had those days when we wondered why we had accomplished so little. But we developed the habit of comparing the real costs of activities or programs—that on the surface seemed "right"—to the likelihood that it would pay off in a significant and timely way.

Yes, some programs that we valued were cut back or dropped, many temporarily, others permanently. Two-week school visits from an artist or scientist were substituted for the assemblies that had consistently fragmented school days. Fund raisers were minimized or dropped. The student photo days that had proliferated were reduced in number. Math Discovery Mornings, where students shared what they learned with parents and family members, took the place of parent math classes.

These decisions were not easy, and changes did not happen overnight. Yet over time we began noticing students who were so excited about solving mathematics problems that they did not want to stop, even for lunch or to go outside. For many children the "work" of mathematics became "play." As more students tasted success, even more began to work harder. And the payoff of all that extra work was that more students became competent and more students blossomed. These student outcomes are possible for all schools, but making hard decisions using the 80/20 Rule is necessary.

Instruction and the 80/20 Rule

In our early years of teaching we had not yet considered the 80/20 Rule. Some days our instruction slowed down as we waited until all students were finished before moving on in class. Sometimes we stalled on one lesson until all the students were successful. We often let our less-experienced students determine the pace for all of our students. As a result, the success of our entire class suffered. It is clear to us now that matching the overall instructional pace to the upper 80 percent of students energizes a class. We believe that all students can succeed, and this translates into high expectations for all students, driving the entire class forward. Yet we do not forget the most needy; students who need additional support receive it through intervention and lesson differentiation.

Differentiation allows teachers to maintain the pace of 80 percent of students who succeed while supporting the 20 percent who may struggle. High-quality instructional practices and understanding content and learning pathways are important for all students, but are imperative for the 20 percent (see Chapters 5, 6, and 7).

For example, partner or group work supports struggling students. Diversity in knowledge levels becomes an asset as students talk and solve problems together, effectively teaching each other different ways of thinking (see Figure 4.1). Sherry finds the value of the coins by arranging them from greatest to least value, and then counting on by tens, fives, and ones. Her partner, Fiona, who prefers to count by tens, begins by grouping the nickels into pairs. When the girls explain their strategies to each other, both girls learn.

Keeping our expectations high is a gift to all of our children. As students' overall success level climbs, less experienced students often work harder than ever—and they realize that work is the key to success.

In schools, social capital should not result just from being a good athlete or a good artist. Student can and do learn to admire and emulate other students who are good at mathematics. When lower-achieving students find themselves in an environment where mathematics has a high degree of social capital, they work harder than ever to be like their friends.

Figure 4.1 When students work as partners, they learn from each other.

The 80/20 Rule

The 80/20 Rule reminds us of the importance of focus. Instead of sprinkling our attention evenly over all the crises that appear at the principal's door, over all students in a class, or over all the teachers in a school, the 80/20 Rule urges us to analyze the costs and potential benefits for any decision that we make. When we spend 80 percent of our time, energy, and resources on things that matter most or things that are more likely to move the system forward, when we make sure that our overall teaching pace does not slow down for the benefit of a few, more students will benefit in the end.

Although there is no easy answer, no "fairy dust," no sure cure for the multiple demands that teachers, coaches, and principals struggle to meet, the 80/20 Rule provides a guiding light, a way to prioritize decisions, and an important way to illuminate what matters most.

The Principal's Perspective

As an administrator I feel like I'm bombarded throughout the day by a multitude of requests and unplanned events. A fire alarm is pulled. A child is sent to the office for disciplinary reasons. A report is due. I constantly ask myself, "How much energy and time do I give each thing?"

I find that my vision for the school—the end that I have in mind—provides the guidance that I need to make my decision. But it is the 80/20 Rule that requires me to examine this decision from a cost-to-benefit perspective. When I operate from this model, I purposefully allocate my time according to 80/20 proportions. Eighty percent of my energy should be devoted to high-benefit activities and 20 percent of my energy must be devoted to lower-benefit activities.

On any given day at my school a number of students are sent to my office. For my school, the time I spend disciplining students on an individual basis has a low benefit to the overall culture. One day I was working with a second-grade teacher and her students on subtraction strategies when I got a call about a student sent to the office for disciplinary reasons. I responded by asking the office staff to send the fourth grader to the second-grade classroom where I was working.

As the student walked through the door, I asked him to sit quietly while the other children and I continued with the lesson. I maintained my focus on the lesson, and when time permitted, I asked the student what he saw the other children doing at that moment. "María was talking about the strategy she used to solve the problem," he said.

Probing further, I asked, "How do you think María learned those strategies?"

The response was a typical one, because of the culture we have created at school: "She did the work."

Then I left the child with that thought as I resumed helping the teacher teach the lesson. This allowed me to spend 80 percent of my time in the following ways:

° Scaffolding student thinking and helping the teacher do the same
° Comparing student work and analyzing the student strategies
° Determining how to engage the students in a discussion about their strategies
° Modeling the whole-group discussion at the end
° Discussing the teacher's next steps

When the lesson was over, I reminded the child, "What are the two most important things in our school?"

The child responded appropriately: "Respect and work."

Then I asked, "Which were you not doing in your classroom?" The child admitted he wasn't working. "You saw the kids working in second grade," I reminded him. "Do you think you're ready to do that work?" I ended by letting the child know that if he was sent to the office again, he'd end up doing his work in that second-grade classroom.

I can handle many discipline situations this same way. An angry child gets to cool off and decompress in a productive classroom. Eighty percent of my energy remains on researching high-quality instruction with a teacher, and 20 percent of my energy is spent on discipline.

The 80/20 Rule was instrumental one April as we worked to create the budget for the following year. The bad news was that we had a significant reduction in our Title I funds. When I heard this news, I reflected using the 80/20 Rule, and did a cost-to-benefit analysis of possible solutions. I concluded that most important for our students was to maintain our successful system of intervention for kindergarten and grade one students. Additionally, it was critical to continue providing professional development for our teachers so that they could keep leveraging the effect that instruction has on children. Unfortunately, to do this we would need to eliminate three teacher assistant positions so that we could keep our outdoor-learning specialist and interventionist positions.

Next I gathered my leadership team, a representative group of teachers and staff, to examine our situation and my conclusions. This leadership group is a high-functioning, representative group of staff members, a think tank with unique perspectives and approaches that is highly focused on students' welfare. Members of this group have a good understanding of the 80/20 Rule and are well acquainted with making decisions with the cost-to-benefit model in mind.

The team analyzed possible ways our school could absorb the cuts, but concluded as well that to maintain the educational gains our students had made, we would need to protect our intervention program—and that three teacher assistant positions would have to be cut. At the same time, the leadership team was very concerned about the reaction of the rest of the staff.

I agreed that the classroom teachers would have a great deal of difficulty with this idea because of their personal relationships with their teacher assistants. During the meeting with the entire staff, I facilitated a conversation that kept the majority of our staff's energy and thinking on what we agreed was most important for our students: maintaining the system of intervention and maintaining our access to high-quality professional development.

First we listed every position that was currently part of the Title I budget. With respect for the hard work and dedication of each individual, we discussed how each position made important contributions to the overall mission of our school.

Then we moved to a cost-to-benefit analysis. We discussed our students, nearly all of whom lived in poverty and arrived at school without initial learning skills. The teachers identified that intervention was key to many students' long-term success in school.

At first, the teachers wanted to give up the physical education teacher. They made comments such as, "We don't need our students to have chances to develop language and physical skills outdoors. We need our teacher assistants to help the students."

Our cost-to-benefit analysis made the conversation more emotionally neutral, and more objective. We listed the benefits of having a physical education teacher, who worked with small groups of kindergarten and grade one students:

- Six teachers were freed to work with two intervention groups of their own students each day. The classroom teachers, who best knew the students and who had the most training in interventions, were the best people to provide intervention services.
- All students had chances to improve their physical health and well-being.
- All students had chances to develop language in the context of outdoor experiences.

Eighty percent of our energy was now on what was most important: the students. In this way the teachers realized that the outdoor-learning specialist was vital to keeping our intervention program intact. They recognized that keeping our teacher assistants had little or no effect on interventions, and that, although they certainly supported instruction, they were not essential.

In the end, a teacher spoke up. "I need to say something. I acknowledge that we need to keep our physical education teacher, but I want to say that my teacher assistant is a valuable person." When the teacher made that statement, other teachers said the same: "We value our aides. But the right thing to do is to maintain the interventions for our children."

The cost-to-benefit model kept the children at the forefront of our discussion and kept our conversation neutral. The relationships that teachers had with their teacher assistants were respected, yet we kept alive the vision of what our task was. The cost-to-benefit analysis neutralized the emotional investment that people had in their colleagues so that an objective decision could be made.

We reassured the teachers that their aides would be supported in finding new jobs, and that we had their best interests at heart. In the end the teacher assistants did find new jobs in other schools. Our teachers made the right decision for their students, and all individuals at the school were taken care of.

The Math Coach's Perspective

I spend a great deal of my time talking with individual teachers about what their students are learning, and the difficulties that students encounter with new concepts. Frequently teacher talk turns to their frustrations—which is completely understandable. Teachers talk about how parents don't support their kids, how students don't bring back homework, and how children forget things over the summer so that teachers have to reteach what the children should already know.

Although I realize that sometimes teachers need to vent their frustrations, I work hard to make sure that the majority of my conversations with them are spent on high-value, reflective discussions. It's that 80/20 Rule. One day after a teacher had vented this way for a while, I knew that I needed to turn the talk toward what she could control. I said with all sincerity, "I hear your frustration about Sandra, because you know that she can do better. I get that, and I know that I'd feel just like you.

"Now," I continued, "let's talk about Carolina. She's part of your eighty percent who can and want to learn. How is she doing? I remember that the last time we met, you were excited about her new strategies for solving number strings. Carolina added $3 + 2 + 7 + 2$ by combining 3 and 7 to get 10, then she added the doubles, and then she knew immediately that $10 + 4 = 14$. Is Carolina using those strategies on a regular basis now? And how are you encouraging that strategy to spread to other students?"

Honoring teachers' needs, but moving conversations toward the eighty percent is key to moving a school forward. It is so easy to get mired in conditions we cannot control! The 80/20 Rule keeps our focus on what is most important: the research that teachers are doing to help students comprehend mathematics.

How do I honor teachers' needs during teacher meetings? I often record their issues in writing.

On the board I wrote "What We Can Expect" as the grade-level meeting veered toward the teachers' very valid complaints. I listed their words beneath the heading:

- Over the summer students forget what they learned the previous year.
- Some children arrive at school late.
- Ninety percent of our kindergartners do not come to school with readiness skills.
- Many families are not taking responsibility for helping their children at home.
- Many children come to school without necessary language skills.

Then I added to the list some other things that we can expect:

- We have most of the children with us for six and a half hours each day.
- Our school has routines for math that are consistent from classroom to classroom, which buys back instructional time at the beginning of the following year.
- Our school has patterns of instruction that are consistent from classroom to classroom, which makes instruction more predictable for children.

"It's true that children don't come to school with necessary language skills," I said, pointing to that bullet on the chart. "And the difficult thing is that students have to be fluent in the language of mathematics if they are to be successful. Students simply cannot engage in classroom discussions without that language. Furthermore students can be extremely capable in mathematics, yet do poorly on mathematics assessments if they cannot understand and use math language.

"What can we do to improve the language skills of our students?" I asked, moving the discussion from what we can't control to what we can control. And the meeting continued in a much more productive manner.

Focusing on the 80 percent—what we could control—allowed me to prevent the 20 percent from dominating our precious professional learning time. As a coach, I made the conscious decision to reinforce the culture of research, which we know leads to academic success. I made the conscious decision to respectfully move the discussion away from an easy conversation to a more challenging conversation that would affect the school culture and had the potential to dramatically change opportunities for children.

The Teacher's Perspective

One of the hardest things for me is that my time with individual students is so very limited. There's only one of me, and there are twenty-five kids. They all are different, they all are six or seven years old, and they all need so much. Not one of my students is reading on grade level. Not one! Even Lucy, my most experienced reader, is below grade level! So how are they going to be able to read the word problems in math? Do I spend most of my spare time on Cally, my neediest student? What about the students who are "almost there"? And do I give up my time with Lucy? Even she is behind where she needs to be!

This is the reality: I have to balance my time as well as I can. The 80/20 Rule reminds me that I need to keep the level of whole-class lessons targeted to what the majority of the kids can do. I have to adjust, or differentiate, as best as I can for Cally within those lessons. Slowing everyone down for Cally is not in her best interests. I do, and will always, give Cally a share of my individual time, but I have to balance that.

As the other kids become independent at reading and math, there will be more competent helpers in my class, and that will help Cally, too. As Cally watches the others do math successfully, she emulates what they do. And she wants to be like the other kids. Her motivation and her willingness to work will pay her big dividends some day. So I differentiate problems for Cally, and I give her a share of my time. But I'm careful to balance my attention with the other students, too.

Menu time, when students revisit activities or games, gives me a chance to pull Cally aside for help or play counting games that are easy for the others. And I'm always careful to pair her with a student with whom she can learn and work.

But it's taken me longer to figure out how to include her during whole-group lessons. This is what I do now:

After I introduce the lesson and give the students a problem to solve, I provide Cally and Susan with a version of the problem that they can do successfully. I let them know that when they finish that version, they should try the problem that I gave the class.

I make sure that I spend the next portion of my time with the more-experienced students. I want to make sure that they use the higher-level strategies that they are capable of, rather than the lower-level counting strategies with which they are very comfortable. That's how I make sure the class discussion will include high-level reasoning that I know some students can and should do. Then I check in with the others. When I can, I pull Cally and Susan aside for help.

There will never be an easy answer for this, and I'm sure over time I'll find better ways to meet Cally's needs. But I do believe that the students who make up my 80 percent need to determine the overall pace of my teaching.

Chapter 5
Patterns of Talk

Words are like eggs: When they are hatched, they have wings.

—Madagascar proverb

Words have power, and—in all schools—words abound.

Talk flows throughout lessons in classrooms, hallway conversations, and meetings large and small. Whether inside the cafeteria or classrooms, on the playground, or in the parking lot, students, teachers, parents, and school staff are constantly communicating with each other—and sometimes about each other.

At Pueblo Gardens Elementary School we worked hard to understand the potential energy of talk. Over time, talk became a low-cost resource that we could leverage to increase the effectiveness of mathematics lessons—and to move the school forward. We also worked to minimize the kind of talk that could pull a school backward or leave it frozen in the status quo.

But first we had to become conscious of our own patterns of talk. In our roles as principal and coach, we paid close attention to meetings, informal chats, and lessons to try to figure out what made one discussion energizing and powerful, and another discussion frustrating and painful.

Over time we learned to capitalize more effectively on these patterns of talk. Although all of our discussions were not—and are not—models of perfection, we came to understand patterns of talk, and as a result a higher percentage of our discussions bore fruit. Leveraging patterns of talk over time helped Pueblo Gardens Elementary School flower into a healthy mathematical learning environment where high-poverty children were able to become highly successful in mathematics.

Patterns of Talk in the Mathematics Classroom

As you observe any mathematics lesson, ask yourself these questions:
Who talks during lessons?
To whom do they talk?
What do they talk about?
How do they talk?

The answers to these questions paint a picture of current patterns of talk, and what and who is valued in a mathematics classroom. The answers also frame possibilities for patterns of talk to unleash the transformation of a classroom, a school, or even a district.

The Ping-Pong Pattern

Talk—or discourse—in mathematics lessons can take on different patterns. Perhaps the most pervasive pattern is the Ping-Pong Pattern, where words fly between the speakers
back and forth,
back and forth,
back and forth.

Although Ping-Pong Patterns of talk are very common, they generally are ineffective. The talk bounces from teacher to student, student to teacher, teacher to student, with teachers asking a question and a single student answering it. Since the teacher is doing the majority of the talk, the teacher is doing most of the learning. Consider the patterns in this ping-pong discussion:

Teacher (referring to Figure 5.1): *What kind of angle is this?*
(Some students raise their hands.)
Teacher: *Sammy?*

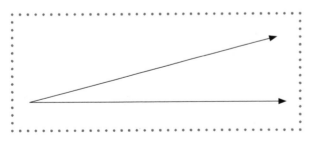

Figure 5.1

Sammy: *Acute.*
Teacher: *That's right.*
(Teacher draws the angle in Figure 5.2.)
Teacher (referring to Figure 5.2): *What kind of angle is this?*
(Some students raise their hands.)
Teacher: *Daniel?*
Daniel: *Obtuse.*
Teacher: *Correct!*

Figure 5.2

You likely are well acquainted with the Ping-Pong Pattern of talk, as it is characteristic of many classroom instructional patterns. Consider why this pattern is less than effective.

You might note that

º the teacher is the source of the right answer.
º the students either know the answer or they don't, and there are no resources to which they can refer.
º one student is engaged at a time. The others are probably relieved to be off the hook, thinking, "I'm so glad the teacher (or principal) didn't call on *me*."
º the teacher or principal is doing most of the talking—and typically whoever is doing the talking is doing most of the learning.

Ping-Pong Patterns often reduce students to guessing the answer that the educator has in mind instead of thinking for themselves. Rather than engaging in ping-pong talk, we ask educators to lay the ping-pong paddle down, take hold of that ball, examine it—and then pass it to the students.

Improved Patterns of Talk

Consider the following discussion and how it differs from the preceding discussion. What patterns of talk do you see? Why are they more effective?

Teacher (referring to Figure 5.3): *You have several plastic triangles labeled with an A in front of you. They're all the same size and shape; they're all congruent.*

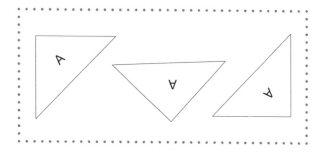

Figure 5.3

Teacher: *Pick up one triangle and examine each of its three angles.*

(Pause.)

Teacher: *Think for yourself: Do you know the measure of any of those angles?*

(Pause.)

Teacher: *Now see whether you and your partner agree on the name of the familiar angle and its measure.*

(Longer pause while students talk.)

Teacher: *Which angle do you immediately know? Hold the triangle up, and point at the angle you are sure of.* (Teacher scans the class.) *Look at your classmates: you all seem to agree about the easy angle. Everybody, please name the angle.*
Students: *Right angle.*
Teacher: *That's correct. And what is its measure?*
Students: *Ninety degrees.*

(Some of the students are looking at the geometry words anchor chart on the wall, using it as a reference. Other students recall this information on their own.)

Teacher: *You're right. . . . The anchor chart reminds some of you that a right angle measures 90 degrees. Can you all say that?*
Students: *A right angle measures 90 degrees.*

(The teacher notices that many of the English language learners stumble over that phrase.)

Teacher: *Please say it one more time: I'd like mathematical language to tumble off your tongue!*
Students: *A right angle measures 90 degrees.*
Teacher: *Thank you. Now I'm curious about the triangle's other two angles. I wonder how you might use what you know about the right angle to figure out the measure of the other two angles. Please think quietly on your own for a bit, and then talk to your partner to see what your partner thinks. Be ready to explain to the class what the measures of the other angles are, and convince us that you're correct.*

(Students pick up the triangles, placing them on top of each other and beside each other to compare the angles. Before long the room is filled with students explaining their thinking, and asking each other questions. Some disagree with each other, but eventually they come to consensus.)

Consider the patterns of talk that are more successful. You might note that

- the teacher builds in individual thinking time.
- the teacher uses choral response, where students answer together as a group. (This is especially important for English language learners but is an engagement strategy for all students.)
- the class wall has a reference chart for important vocabulary, and the teacher encourages students to use that chart.
- the teacher has partners talk to each other, often after quiet think time. (This is often called "think-pair-share.")
- students are asked to solve problems and come up with convincing arguments that support their ideas.

Now examine how the whole-class discussion continues:

Teacher: *Jordan and Daniel, would you please share with the group what you first discovered?*

(While the students were working on the problem, the teacher had noticed that the boys had clear and convincing proof that the angles are congruent. At that time she asked whether they would be willing to share this with the class.)

Jordan: *I know that the two angles are the same. They go on top of each other, like they're con . . . congruent.*

(Jordan comes up to the overhead. He places two triangles on top of each other, matching up the acute angles. Then he flips the top triangle horizontally. The pieces fit perfectly to prove that the two acute angles are congruent.)

(Jordan looks up at the teacher for confirmation.)

Teacher: *Remember: you're talking to the class, not to me, about how you knew the angles were the same. Do the others agree with you?*
Jordan (looking at the class): *Do you agree?*

Lindsey: *We said the same, 'cause they look the same.*
Daniel: *They hafta be the same 'cause they match.*
Teacher: *What has to be the same?*
Daniel: *The angles.*
Teacher: *The angles have to . . .*
Daniel: *The angles have to be the same.*
Jordan: *Congruent, they're congruent 'cause they fit on top.*
Teacher: *I'm glad to hear that mathematical term* congruent. *Let's all say it together.*
Class: *Congruent.*

Paula: *And we know the degrees. It's 45.*
Teacher: *Convince us.*

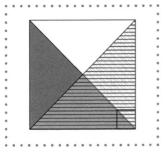

(Paula and Herbert come up to the overhead and place three triangles on it; see Figure 5.4.)

Paula: *See, the two acute angles fit into the right angle. Since the right angle is 90 degrees, you just divide it and you get 45.*
Kerrey: *I don't get it.*
Herbert: *The 90 degrees is in half of each angle, so 45 + 45 = 90.*
Teacher: *This is important thinking. Jason, please explain what Herbert said in your own words.*

Figure 5.4 Paula and Herbert use manipulatives to prove the measurement of the acute angles.

Consider the patterns of talk that are most successful. You might note that

- the teacher orchestrated the initial discussion. She listened to the students as they worked, identified how she would begin the discussion, and asked them if they would be willing to share. This allowed the students to plan ahead, and even rehearse what they would say.
- the teacher encouraged the students to talk to the class, rather than to her, which encouraged a discussion between the students.
- the teacher highlighted important thinking by having other students restate other people's ideas.
- the teacher encouraged the students to speak in complete sentences and use mathematical terminology.
- the students are the source of the right answer rather than the teacher, and high-quality thinking rather than a textbook answer key is the proof.
- the teacher kept the focus of the discussion on the student thinking, but also encouraged the use of correct terminology.

Now examine how the classroom discussion continues:

Teacher: *Does anyone have a different way to prove the measurement of those acute angles?*

(Donna and Nina come up to the overhead. They place eight triangles so the acute angles rotate around a single point; see Figure 5.5.)

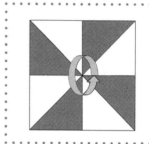

Figure 5.5 Nina uses what she knows about 360 degrees to figure out the measurement of the acute angle.

Donna: *Nina and I did this circle. And we know that they all rotate and make 360 degrees, and that makes the angles 40.*
Nina: *It's like 360 divided by 8.* (She writes the division problem and uses long division, but she makes an error in her division and comes up with 40. She looks up, confused, as she rethinks her answer.) *Is it 40 or 45?*
Teacher: *Nina is questioning her answer. Please talk to your partner and see what you think. Does 360 divided by 8 equal 40? If not, what is the quotient? And how do you know that you're right?*

Now consider the patterns of talk that were most successful. You might note that
- the teacher encouraged multiple proofs and more than one way to solve a problem.
- errors were not perceived as unfortunate mistakes, but were instead presented as an opportunity to examine an idea. Students were free to change their minds when new evidence came to light.

Without a doubt, patterns of talk within classrooms have a considerable effect on student learning. In the same way, patterns of talk among adults significantly influence a school's ability to change its mathematics culture.

Patterns of Talk Between Adults

The ineffective Ping-Pong Pattern of talk is not confined to classroom discussions. It also bounces its way through staff meetings and hallway conversations, and is especially rampant during disagreements.

Mr. Thomas: *The district has the most ridiculous pacing calendar.*
Ms. Watson: *I think the teachers really need it.*

Mr. Thomas: *But it moves way too fast.*

Ms. Watson: *But so many teachers get to testing time and find that they haven't even covered important things like fractions.*

Mr. Thomas: *It's a big problem. It drives me crazy.*

Ms. Watson: *But not everyone is the same as you.*

Mr. Thomas: *The district just keeps piling ridiculous things on us.*

Ms. Watson: *I know, but . . .*

Holding the Ball

What if the preceding discussion didn't ping-pong back and forth, but one speaker "held the ball"? What if one or both speakers chose to really listen to the other, to seek to understand the other's perspective? What if a speaker asked the other for clarification, perhaps by paraphrasing or restating what the other said? How might the conversation sound?

Mr. Thomas: *The district has the most ridiculous math pacing calendar!*

Ms. Watson: *It sounds like the pacing calendar is a really big problem to you.*

Mr. Thomas: *It* is *a problem. It moves way too fast.*

Ms. Watson: *Tell me more.*

Mr. Thomas: *We barely began fractions when the calendar said to move on to decimals. The kids weren't ready.*

Ms. Watson: *Hmm . . . (Pause, nodding.) I see what you mean. The calendar tells you to move on, but you know it's not the right thing for your kids. That* is *a problem.*

Mr. Thomas: *That happened when I was working on geometry, too, but during that unit the kids didn't need as much time as the calendar said.*

Ms. Watson: *So the calendar sometimes goes too fast and sometimes goes too slowly. There's no way that one calendar can match what all students need.*

Mr. Thomas: *That's what I'm saying.*

Ms. Watson: *So what's wrong with taking the pacing calendar as a guide, as a suggestion? That's how I see it. I think that's what a pacing calendar is there for, to help us make sure that when test time comes, we've covered everything. I just don't see it as a lockstep day-by-day requirement.*

Holding the Ball requires the speaker to be present and focused on the other person. Think of any teacher whom you admire and who is a very effective teacher, and you'll find that these people all have a characteristic in common: they exercise the ability to be in the present moment.

"I had a great 'teachable moment'!" is a statement that illustrates "Holding the Ball." During a teachable moment the teacher, coach, or principal focuses on what students say, and uses that information to drive the direction of a lesson. During a teachable moment a lesson plan becomes a map rather than a rigid structure. During a teachable moment, students' voices are heard, and their ideas are respected, while the teacher capitalizes on the strengths that a community of learners provides. Teachers facilitate, guiding outcomes that are both planned and spontaneous.

Assuming the Best

Many a conversation between children, between adults and children, and between adults has been waylaid by people assuming the worst.

What if, instead, the speaker assumed the best? What if, up front, a student assumed that the other child stepped on his foot by accident rather than on purpose? What if the teacher assumed that the child did her homework and forgot it, rather than that she was "lazy" and didn't do it at all? What if a principal assumed that a frustrated teacher was trying his best and just needed support with a difficult group of students?

Assuming the Best is a highly effective pattern based on the fact that, indeed, most principals, teachers, coaches, and children really want to do the right thing. Most people do the best that they can at any moment. And everybody makes mistakes. Assuming the best moves conversations away from the blame game, a pattern that maintains "what is." Assuming the best moves conversations into the realm of problem solving and the promise of possibility.

There Is No "They"

In how many conversations in schools are "they" responsible?

> "They won't let us do what we need to do."
> "They give us more to do and never take anything away."
> "They think there are more than twenty-four hours in a day."
> "They don't understand what it's like in a classroom."

We believe that there is no "they"—at least not in the way that many principals, teachers, and coaches might think. "They" is whoever educators believe is in control and making poor decisions: perhaps the superintendent or central office personnel, the principal, or a lead teacher.

We know that, at the end of the day, each educator has the power to make many choices. True, there is paperwork that has to be completed, and requirements that seem to increase rather than decrease. True, there are many things that are not the way we think they should be. This will always be the case.

That being said, each educator has the power to make most of the decisions over how he or she will spend the next seven hours with his or her students, the next thirty minutes during a conference with a teacher, or the next five minutes on the phone with a parent.

More important than what "they" do is what *we* will do, and how we will do it. Looking into the eyes of children, trying to see the world through those eyes, feel what they feel, and understand why they do what they do gives us the patience and strength to work through their confusion.

Looking into the eyes of teachers, coaches, or principals, trying to see the world through those eyes, feel their concerns, and understand why they make those decisions gives us the patience and strength to help them move beyond the boundaries of how they have taught or made decisions in the past.

There is no "they" that stops you from doing the right thing. You, not "they," are in control.

Downward-Spiraling Talk

Education is probably one of the most difficult professions that there is. When educators look in the mirror, they see their reflections sporting the hats of social worker, psychologist, and doctor. They are also asked to be personal trainers for academics, sports, and the arts, as well as for developing manners, kindness, and how to work with partners. Expectations rise while resources fall.

To leverage talk for school change, conversations cannot continually perch in the "Ain't It Awful" category. Yes, venting is fine, and even necessary. But continual venting without focusing on actions leads to talk that spirals lower and lower. In contrast, leveraged talk means that venting moves on to "What Can I Do?"

Educators are strongly concerned about the students who are "outliers," who are especially needy in academics, behavior, or social skills. This will always be true. However, principals, coaches, and teachers must try to focus closer to 80 percent of their talk on the 80 percent of the students who can and want to do the work, rather than the opposite.

After hearing a teacher talk about how "the kids aren't getting it," another teacher, the coach, or the principal must ask, "About what percent have difficulty? About half? More than half?"

These clarification questions move the conversation from general to specific, from nebulousness to data. These questions also move the speaker into a problem-solving stance that requires him or her to consider how the 80 percent are doing. And it's the status of the 80 percent of the students that determines whether the initial classroom instruction was effective. It's the 80 percent that should guide the teacher's whole-group decision making, and so should occupy the majority of his or her thinking. This moves teachers from a state of limitations to a state of possibility.

Asking Hard Questions

There have always been questions that are hard to ask, and there always will be. Most of these questions have to do with student outcomes.

"We did a whole unit on decimals, and the kids still think that 3.15 is more than 3.9," a principal mourns. Educators often echo similar words of disappointment.

Students have difficulties because much of mathematics can be very nebulous. Many students understand content when they use visual models and when they are allowed to make sense of it themselves. When the same idea is expressed with numbers and equations, it can be hard for many students to make the leap to abstraction. For example, educators would do well to keep the fraction equivalency strips available to students throughout the fraction unit, even when more of the work is being done with fraction notation.

Often the problem is bridging from visible, concrete models to abstract numbers and equations, and keeping the bridge available to students who need it.

Principals, coaches, and teachers must continually ask whether students understand. They must gather that data throughout lessons and units, and then respond to that data. When educators do not ask this hard question, a superficial Band-Aid hides serious misconceptions that will surely be problematic for students as more-complex mathematics is layered on top of weakness.

Other hard questions must be asked of teachers, coaches, and principals:

"Can I help you understand why the algorithm for multiplying fractions asks students to multiply both the numerator and the denominator?"

If the teacher, coach, or principal does not understand the mathematics they are teaching, how can their students?

"Your students still talk about the '2' in '27' as a '2.' What is causing that, and what action can we take so that they use place value when they are computing?"

Educators worry when students don't comprehend when reading; they should be equally concerned when students don't comprehend while doing mathematics.

"Half of my students came into my class knowing their combinations of 10. The other half seem to not even understand what combinations are. Imagine how much more efficient we could be as a school if we were more consistent. How can we make that happen?"

One of the most effective leverage points for schools is to have consistent expectations between classrooms within a grade and from grade to grade.

"I notice that your students' accuracy is consistently lower than the other third graders. Why might this be? What can we do about it?"

Discussions about student outcomes are critical and necessary. But notice the "we" in the questions:

We *are owning this problem.*
We *will work to understand the problem and research solutions.*
And we *will solve this problem together.*

Insights, Next Steps, By When

One of the patterns of talk that makes the most significant difference in our work at schools is how we end meetings and important conversations. Just as lessons have three parts—an introduction, an investigation, and a summary—so do meetings.

It is common to begin a meeting by identifying its goals and purpose. The new pattern that we adopted was to end meetings with three steps:

1. First, we summarize by sharing the most important insights from that meeting.
2. Then we clearly articulate our "next steps," or what we will commit to doing differently as a result of the meeting.
3. Last we create a "by when" statement, which gives us a time line to which we will hold ourselves accountable.

Before we started ending meetings in this systematic way, we would end simply by thanking people for coming. When our patterns for ending meetings changed, we consistently summarized our most important insights. In so doing, we had to revisit the path that the meeting took and determine what was most essential to us. The "next steps" ensured that we made a commitment to visible, important changes. And the "by when" gave us a date to aim for and made us accountable for making those commitments a reality. These specifics were noted and became check-in points for subsequent meetings. "Insights," "next steps," and "by when" made it more likely that meeting notes wouldn't slide directly into files and disappear into oblivion. These patterns provided the structure that transformed "good ideas" into steps toward reality.

Don't Take Yourselves Too Seriously

Schooling is serious business, especially in schools that are the main hope, perhaps the only hope, for high-poverty children or for students whose first language is not English. At the same time, it is important to keep perspective. In the cryptic yet wise words of a Zen master, "It matters a lot; it matters not at all."

Keeping balance in our lives, valuing our small but consistent steps toward change, and laughing at the precious moments that come our way make the journey manageable, interesting, and fun. Inviting others to share in our successes is not only regenerating, but also creates the school we all want to be.

A fifth grader was listening to a first grader, LaShonda, happily read the word problems she wrote. LaShonda smiled, and said with wide eyes, "My heart is bumping for no reason!"

We smiled.

Second graders Micah and Felicia were using coins to find different ways to make 23 cents. Toward the end of the lesson they examined the ten equations that they had written. They looked at each other, amazed and surprised: "We got 23 on all of them!"

We educators looked at each other in amazement, perplexed that the students were surprised that the sum was always 23. We laughed.

Silly puns, grinning at your own mistakes, gently teasing the kids and each other . . . . Whatever you do, make the journey enjoyable.

Patterns of Talk

Patterns of talk have powerful potential for leveraging school change. Throughout the school, it is talk that either maintains the current school's culture and values or brings to life a new system of beliefs.

Capitalize on the power of talk to transform your mathematics program. For words truly are like eggs—when they hatch, they have wings.

The Principal's Perspective

I remember when I first started going into classrooms with my clipboard in hand and a checklist. It was easy and efficient, and my life as a principal was about tight observation schedules. When it came to doing evaluations, I followed the district protocols and knew the routines very well. I remember talking with a group of principals about how many "evals" they had done.

Since then I have learned to leverage the informal conversations that I have with teachers, coaches, parents, and students, and I use my time very differently. I systematically talk with people to motivate them, but not in the sense of a cheerleader. In a very intentional manner I try to understand, and sometimes change, how people think. With students, I work to elevate their ideas to a more mature level.

I was working on a lesson about possible combinations that students could make, given three kinds of drinks and two kinds of fruit. The lesson in the curriculum was relatively straightforward, and the students easily created a matrix of possible combinations (Figure 5.6).

	Milk	Juice	Water
Apples	Milk Apples	Juice Apples	Water Apples
Bananas	Milk Bananas	Juice Bananas	Water Bananas

Figure 5.6 This matrix helped the students organize their thinking about combinations.

"Thanks for joining us," began Ms. Davis, ready to finish up the lesson. I looked Ms. Davis in the eye and smiled, and she knew that I had an idea up my sleeve.

"I was wondering," I said to the class, "what would happen if we included another set in our combinations. What if we decided to have two kinds of cereal in our breakfast?"

The students' eyes lit up as they imagined this new scenario. "Woo-hoo!" "Wow!" and "Awesome!" rang out from the group.

"So what two kinds of cereal would you like to include?" I asked. "Talk to your partner about what two cereals we could have." I know how choices engage students, and for a moment Ms. Davis and I watched the lively discussions.

"Now I need to think," Ms. Davis said, laughing. "I know how to use a tree diagram to include a third set. But a matrix? I don't think so!"

Ms. Davis retrieved a piece of scratch paper to draw her tree diagram.

I called the students back together, and they decided to include Froot Loops and Lucky Charms. I wrote those cereal names on the board.

"So now how many different combinations could we have? What would they be? And can a matrix help us keep track of them?"

I paused, to let the students have some quiet think time. Then I repeated their task. "Please turn to your partner. How many different combinations of drinks, fruit, and cereal would we have now? And how can the matrix help you?"

Some students retrieved whiteboards and began sketching, and the others pointed at the matrix on the board. Their faces were animated, and discussion filled the room.

After a few minutes, I pulled the students back together. "What do you think?" I inquired.

I asked Kiera and Jonathan to place their whiteboard on the document camera so the class could see it.

"We just put two little parts inside each box," Kiera explained. (See Figure 5.7.)

"Each box shows the cereal," Jonathan said. "Then you count the little boxes to in …indicate all the different ways." Jonathan tried out an academic term that his teacher had introduced.

Javier and Claire adapted the matrix in a different way. Along the

	Milk	Juice	Water
Apples	Milk Apples ☐ ☐	Juice Apples ☐ ☐	Water Apples ☐ ☐
Bananas	Milk Bananas ☐ ☐	Juice Bananas ☐ ☐	Water Bananas ☐ ☐

Figure 5.7 Kiera and Jonathan drew boxes inside the matrix as a pictorial way to keep track of the new combinations.

top they listed the two-item sets that the class had previously identified. Because of my scaffolding, they made a new matrix with all the possible combinations that included Froot Loops and Lucky Charms (Figure 5.8).

	Milk Apples	Juice Apples	Water Apples	Milk Bananas	Juice Bananas	Water Bananas
Froot Loops	Milk Apples **Froot Loops**	Juice Apples **Froot Loops**	Water Apples **Froot Loops**	Milk Bananas **Froot Loops**	Juice Bananas **Froot Loops**	Water Bananas **Froot Loops**
Lucky Charms	Milk Apples **Lucky Charms**	Juice Apples **Lucky Charms**	Water Apples **Lucky Charms**	Milk Bananas **Lucky Charms**	Juice Bananas **Lucky Charms**	Water Bananas **Lucky Charms**

Figure 5.8 "There are six more combinations when you add Lucky Charms and Froot Loops," David told Claire.

After the lesson ended, the children went off to lunch with visions of food combinations dancing in their heads. "Think about new combination problems that you can do with today's lunch!" I called after them.

Ms. Davis smiled. "I learned from the kids today," she said. "And it was well worth the extra time we spent."

That day Ms. Davis saw me use talk to challenge students to a higher level. Other days she might see me struggle with student misunderstandings. In either case, my work in classrooms allows me to talk authentically with teachers.

The Math Coach's Perspective

I was so pleased about the coaching debriefing that I did today! I realized that I'm internalizing patterns of talk for coaching, and that these patterns really work.

First of all, Lucy is a wonderful teacher, very reflective and always thinking about what she can do to help the kids be more successful. While she was teaching, I "whisper coached," which means that although Lucy did most of the lesson, I gave her suggestions as it progressed. I taught small portions of the lesson, but Lucy did the bulk of it.

I noticed that the objective that she shared with the students at the beginning of the lesson did not match what she was teaching. I told her that the kids were not "measuring items that are a centimeter or an inch," but were instead "creating benchmarks" for those units.

We quickly conferred while the students worked, and I explained that the purpose of benchmarks is for students to be able to tell themselves, "Yes, I know how long an inch is. It's about the length of my knuckle." Then they can use that as a reference when they think about inches.

Lucy's discussion with the class at the end of the lesson was brilliant! She began by clarifying the lesson's focus. She explained to the students how benchmarks for these units would help them remember the sizes of the units.

The students shared their benchmarks for an inch, a foot, and a yard. Then Lucy asked them to select the benchmark that they thought would most help them remember the size of each unit. Uyen chose the diameter of a marker to remind her of an inch, and Julia chose the width of the hundred chart to remind her of a yard.

At the end of the lesson, Lucy and I met to debrief. I began the debriefing by using a pattern of talk that I have found especially effective. Just as I begin math lessons with an introduction or identification of the lesson focus, I start lesson debriefings by having the teacher select the focus.

I began by thanking Lucy for inviting me into her classroom, and I told her how much I enjoyed her lesson. I shared a few things that she did that I was going to try to include in my own teaching. Not only was this comment in the true spirit of research, but it also made clear that I believe that she's a good teacher. This validation is important; I often notice that the best teachers question their abilities the most.

Next I asked Lucy how our discussion could be most helpful to her. She said, "I've always struggled with measurement. It always seemed so complicated and so vague to me. I'd like to make sense of what is important in measurement."

"That's a good idea," I responded. "It is helpful to be clear about important big ideas, and measurement is complex." I paraphrased what she said—another pattern of talk that I use quite a bit as a coach.

We talked about the important role that benchmarks play in measurement. "I thought they were more for estimating," Lucy told me. "Now I see that they help students recall the size of units."

"That's right," I agreed. "It seems to me that today's lesson brought them to the awareness level. In tomorrow's lesson you'll have them consciously select a benchmark that will help them. Then during later experiences the children will consolidate those ideas."

I shared with Lucy some other teaching moves she had made that were extremely effective, moves that are explained in detail in *Classroom Discussions* (Chapin et al. 2009). I know that positive, specific feedback often increases teachers' use of that technique.

"You asked Lonnie to revoice what Hadley said," I told her. "When you asked him to restate her comment, the whole class sat up straight and paid closer attention."

Lucy glowed. "It did work!" she commented. "I've been working on revoicing. The other students feel like they are going to be called upon, so it makes them more accountable."

"I noticed that, too," I said. "And the more you use revoicing, the more accountable the students will be. Soon it will become a habit for them."

I went on to share with her another positive move that she consistently made. "You asked for specific and precise language," I said. "When a student said that the faucet was about an inch, you asked him to explain which part of the faucet he was referring to. And when he said, 'The faucet,' you asked whether he meant the length or the width."

I then explained the importance of this.

"Mathematics is a language that is precise and specific. One example is how we read word problems. It's very different from how we read a novel. When we read a novel, we can skip words or even sentences and still comprehend the bulk of the story. But when we read a word problem, every single word matters. They have to understand every single part of it, as well as the relationships between each part of the word problem."

Lucy's eyes widened in recognition of what I had said. "I see," she said. "Thanks for telling me that. Now I can be more explicit about that with the kids."

I ended our conversation by asking her what about our conversation was most helpful to her. She answered, "This makes me feel more confident. Now I know that benchmarks are items that should pop into their minds when they hear the name of a unit. It's so much more concrete for me now, and I'll continue with the lesson tomorrow and highlight that idea. Thanks!"

The Teacher's Perspective

I often find myself feeling conflicted when talking to other teachers. I'm new here. I have my own set of beliefs, and they don't always match what the other teachers think. The struggle is about how to keep true to myself while making sure that the other teachers see me as "one of them." After all, I need them to be allies. Who else is going to tell me things like how to find cardstock or whether the librarian is flexible about changing schedules?

This conflict, between what I want to say and what I think I can say, surfaced the first day I came to the school. It was a month after school had started. A teacher suddenly had to move out of the state, and I was hired to take over her classroom. The day before I took over, I got the chance to observe the classroom.

I walked in the door and immediately looked around for Roderick, the boy I had been warned about by numerous people—by his current teacher, the reading teacher, the lunch ladies, the custodian, and all the teachers on the kindergarten and first-grade teams. It seemed like everyone at the school knew Roderick.

"He never listens."

"Roderick bullies the other kids."

"He's really a problem kid," his kindergarten teacher told me. "In fact we promoted him only because we didn't want the new kindergartners to have to deal with his behavior."

"Just send him to suspension," another teacher advised. "He won't hurt anyone there." When I walked into the room, it didn't take long for me to pick him out from the rest of the first graders. Within five minutes of my coming in, this six-year-old jumped out of his seat, ran across the room, punched another child, threw three pencils in the air, and then sat under his desk, making fun of the other kids.

It was tempting to write this kid off. But of course I didn't. I took matters into my own hands.

That afternoon Roderick wasn't allowed to play during recess. I sat down on the grass next to him and looked straight into his eyes. "I saw how you behaved today," I told him firmly. "That's the last time you're going to do that. You will listen to me. You will follow my directions. And I'm not going to have to ask you twice."

Roderick nodded. Then he asked, "How do grass grow?"

We talked about seeds and sun and water, and soon Roderick was telling me about his brothers and cousins and the rough way they played at home. I think that we made a much-needed personal connection, which was important.

When I took over the class, I was very clear with him about what I expected of him. I was also very positive with him: when I wanted an example of what was going well, I called on him, and he basked in the glow of positive attention. At the same time, when he pushed limits, as he inevitably did, I gave him immediate consequences.

Before long Roderick was a different child. He finished his work most of the time, he was polite, and he became my best helper.

A few weeks later I was walking down the hall next to the kindergarten teacher he had had the previous year. "Good luck with that Roderick," she said, frowning, and she recited the litany of things that Roderick had done to hurt kids.

I wrestled with my choices: I could say nothing and let this veteran teacher be right. But if I did, these rumors about him would just keep circulating, and he'd always be "That Roderick."

Or I could let people know about his successes—but I knew this teacher didn't want to hear that.

I began by paraphrasing what the teacher had said: "Yeah, I know that he used to hit kids and was really defiant. I definitely saw him do that before I took over. It was amazing that such a little kid had so much power to disrupt things."

"Boy, he sure did that," the teacher agreed.

Then I continued, adding in my new perspective.

"But, I'm seeing new things. Do you know he was the first to pick up Halia when she fell last week? Roderick just went right over and helped her right up. And he got the highest grade on the math test this week. I really think he'll pull it together this year."

"I hope it lasts," the teacher commented, and I could tell from her expression that she didn't expect it to.

I felt good that I had negotiated that conversation in a way that gave Roderick a chance. I said what needed to be said, but I think I did it in a way that respected the other teacher's perspective.

Chapter 6
Patterns in Content

To understand is to perceive patterns.

—Sir Isaiah Berlin

Our preferred seat on a plane is the window seat—to capture the changing view. As the plane leaps from the ground, random trucks, warehouses, and, in Tucson, the occasional tree catch our attention. As the plane circles up and around the city, the busy-ness of city life coalesces into fixed patterns of streets and houses. Human-created patterns eventually give way to nature's mountains and hills and rocks, patterns that look similar at different scales, as do the mingling trickles of water that converge into streams and rivers. As Sir Isaiah Berlin notes, the patterns that we perceive are a window into the relationships around us.

Think of how you use patterns to find your way as you drive in unfamiliar cities. You depend on your GPS device with its friendly voice dispensing advice . . . until it no longer works. Recent construction blocks your path, or a confused machine suggests that you drive the wrong way on a one-way street. Then, understanding the city layouts and street patterns becomes your mental model and only tool.

The GPS voice mirrors the way many teachers teach mathematics: by telling procedure after procedure, similar to the step-by-step progression through the pages of a textbook, grade after grade.

This safe drive through the textbook is typical of mathematics classrooms in the United States. Not only is it easier for teachers to manage, but its framework usually prevents students from asking "those questions," questions that some teachers may not know how to answer, such as "Why does that work?" and "When will I ever use this in life?"

As educators learn about patterns in math content and how those ideas interconnect, decisions about curriculum made on autopilot turn into conscious choices based on student understanding. The more educators recognize the patterns in the mathematical landscape, the more responsive they can be to their students, and the more likely their students will encounter rich experiences that otherwise would have been hidden from view.

Where We Are Today

Liping Ma, a mathematics education researcher, unveils the fragility of teacher mathematics knowledge in her book *Knowing and Teaching Elementary Mathematics: Teachers' Understanding of Fundamental Mathematics in China and the United States* (1999). Ma's unique background, first as a teacher in China and then as an educational researcher in the United States, brought her face-to-face with differences in mathematics instruction that have little to do with culture and everything to do with teachers' understanding of math content.

When Ma first observed classrooms in the United States, she was struck by the difference in how U.S. teachers approach mathematics instruction. She delved into this as a point of research, and discovered that the majority of the teachers in her research sample understood mathematics as a collection of disconnected procedures (107). In contrast, the teachers in her Chinese sample more often talked about mathematics in terms of coherent, interconnected ideas. The Chinese teachers referred to networks of related ideas as "knowledge packages." Chinese teachers also encouraged multiple strategies for solving problems (111). Ma summarized her findings about teacher knowledge of subtraction with regrouping:

> Seventy-seven percent of the U.S. teachers and 14% of the Chinese teachers displayed only procedural knowledge of the topic. Their understanding was limited to surface aspects of the algorithm—the taking and changing steps. This limitation in their knowledge confined their expectations of student learning as well as their capacity to promote conceptual learning in the classroom. (27)

Many of the Chinese teachers clearly articulated the important idea that each larger unit in place value has ten times the value of the preceding unit. They spoke of how important it was for students to regroup numbers in different ways: 42 can be 40 + 2, 30 + 12, 30 + 10 + 2, and so on. Furthermore, many Chinese teachers described different strategies for subtraction and situations where these strategies might be the easiest way to solve a problem (10–15).

Ma likens the "profound understanding of elementary mathematics" that teachers need to an experienced taxi driver who knows multiple avenues for getting to destinations and can be flexible in choosing routes based on the time of day or driving conditions (123).

When educators in any nation are clear about what they are teaching and how best to teach it, students benefit. When educators are uncertain about the important aspects of the mathematics they are teaching, student understanding is at best superficial. A thin veneer of understanding predictably shatters under the pressure of mounting expectations when students progress through the grades. However, when students build a solid understanding of fundamental ideas, they have an enduring support system that can carry the weight of more-complex mathematics over the years.

Knowledge Packages

In our work with principals, coaches, and teachers over the years, we have found that Liping Ma's "knowledge packages" provide educators with a useful way to clarify the ideas that students must understand in mathematics content. Mathematics standards are typically listed in linear form. They tend to reduce mathematics to disconnected lists of knowledge and skills. In contrast, knowledge packages highlight connections between and among ideas. Knowledge packages provide the context and the glue for mathematics standards, bringing ideas together into a more comprehensible whole.

Ma acknowledges that there are various ways that a knowledge package for any given topic might be arranged. Here we describe one pattern for understanding mathematics content that we have used successfully with principals, coaches, and teachers.

For us, knowledge packages may address a large topic, such as multiplication, or describe a task within a topic, such as comparing fractions. The specific contents of a knowledge package vary according to the grade or developmental level being addressed.

To us, knowledge packages contain the following five aspects:
° Concepts: What big overarching ideas for that topic are foundational for student understanding?
° Skills: Which facts or procedures will help students solve problems fluently and efficiently?

- ○ Representations: Which visual models will make concepts and relationships most clearly visible?
- ○ Strategies: Which approaches for accomplishing a task will help students make sense of the mathematics they are learning?
- ○ Mathematical Language: What mathematics vocabulary, terminology, or phrases will allow students to participate in classroom discussions about this topic?

When principals, coaches, and teachers organize their thinking about a mathematics topic in this way, they have a structure for asking these same five questions for all mathematics topics. These categories allow educators to understand what is important for students to know, to teach with clarity and intentionality, and then to assess student understanding with minimal ambiguity. Knowledge packages provide an important pattern for learning and teaching mathematics.

An Example of a Knowledge Package

The following is an example of a knowledge package that a team of grade three teachers developed at one school:

Multiplication for Grade Three
Concepts: ○ Multiplication is combining equal groups.   ○ The number of groups and the number in each group must be considered.   ○ Multiplication is related to division: in division equal groups are removed.   ○ Multiplication has attributes that describe how it works: commutative property, associative property, distributive property.
Skills: ○ Skip-counting by 2, 3, 4, 5, 10   ○ Internalization of multiplication facts with products to 12: 2s, 3s, 4s, 5s, other related facts. Internalization happens as students use factors they know to figure out what they don't know.
Representations: ○ Equal sets   ○ Arrays   ○ Number line

Strategies:
- ° Repeated addition or skip-counting: *"To find 4 × 4, I can count by fours: 4, 8, 12, 16."*
- ° Use relationships: *"I know 2 × 4 = 8, so 4 × 4 must be twice that, or 16."*
- ° Reorder the factors (commutative property): *"3 × 7 = 21, so 7 × 3 must be 21."*
- ° Break apart or "decompose" arrays (distributive property of multiplication over addition)

"To figure out 4 × 7, I can break the array into two smaller arrays that I know: 2 × 7 and 2 × 7."

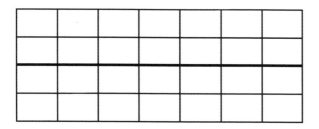

Mathematical Language:
Equal groups, each, factor, product, array, row, skip-count

Knowledge packages are not static words on a page, but instead are the focus of sometimes hotly debated discussions as teachers discuss relationships between standards, prioritize ideas, and seek out new and better ways to teach their students. Schools may differ in the specifics of their knowledge packages, perhaps by including different representations or selecting other vocabulary. But knowledge packages for any operation must include meaningful strategies for computation, such as the multiplication strategy of breaking apart arrays . . . The distributive property in action!

Strategy Example: The Distributive Property in Action

An eighth-grade algebra teacher taught her students a procedure to solve for *n* in the following problem:

$$4 (2n + 6) = 42$$

The teacher told the class, "To solve for n in $4(2n + 6) = 42$, you must multiply the number on the outside (4) by both of the numbers inside the parentheses ($2n$ and 6)." She did several examples of this on the board, and had the students work on similar problems while she monitored their work.

Danira was a capable student, and she quickly began to solve the page of similar problems. However, she consistently multiplied the number outside the parentheses by only one of the numbers inside the parentheses.

For the example on the board Danira wrote $4(2n + 6) = 8n + 6 = 42$ and ended up with $n = \frac{36}{8} = 4\frac{1}{2}$. The answer puzzled her, because when she substituted it for n in the original problem, she didn't get 42. "But that's how you have to do it," Danira said, perplexed.

The coach realized that Danira was making errors partly because this procedure held no meaning for her. "This is what is happening," the coach said, and he drew a 3 × 7 dot array to model a similar problem. Then he divided the array into two parts:

"You can describe this array as 3(7) or as 3(5 + 2)," the coach explained, and Danira nodded.

"Here is another way to show the parts," the coach continued, and he wrote (3 × 5) + (3 × 2), pointing to the two smaller rectangles that the numbers described. "When you add 15 and 6, you get 21, which is the real total of dots. But if you just write (3 × 5) and then add 2, you won't be including all the dots and you'll get only 17. That's why, in your problem, you have to multiply 4 times $2n$, and 4 times 6, and then add both parts together."

Danira's eyes lit up with understanding. "Now I see it!" she said. And this was literally true; the visual model allowed her to see, and then understand, what previously was a procedure that she had merely tried to memorize.

The idea that the distributive property of multiplication over addition could be more than a procedure to memorize was new to the teacher, probably since she herself had learned this as a procedure devoid of meaning. "I've never seen that before," she admitted. "That's neat."

Although it is exciting to see both Danira and her teacher come to a new understanding, it is unfortunate that this idea is not commonly understood by educators. The distributive property should be incorporated as a strategy for learning basic multiplication combinations. Since 7 × 6 is frequently difficult for students who often know 6 × 6, students can use the combination that they know to recall one they don't know.

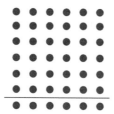

"I know that 6 × 6 = 36, so 7 × 6 must equal 42."

Teachers who think in terms of knowledge packages understand the key roles that concepts, skills, strategies, visual models, and language all play in math content. Teachers who think in terms of knowledge packages learn to seek out these specific aspects of content as they work to better understand the mathematics that they teach.

Knowledge Packages and Systemic Change

Principals have the difficult task of evaluating and supporting instruction of all content areas for many different grades. When they understand the organization of knowledge packages for some mathematics topics in some grades, they can use this structure to initiate content discussions with all teachers of mathematics.

Ms. Garcia, a principal we have worked with, has made time in her schedule to coteach a unit on multiplication with a third-grade teacher. In her research she found that the knowledge package structure guides her thinking as she observes the classroom teacher. Knowledge packages remind her what is important to "chase after" as she teaches lessons. Furthermore, when Ms. Garcia encounters those third-grade students in the cafeteria, she recalls the knowledge package for multiplication and asks the students, "What's the most important thing to remember about multiplication?" She hopes they say something similar to "Multiplication is putting together equal groups, like 6 and 6 and 6 is 18."

Ms. Garcia recently decided to initiate a discussion about content with a fifth-grade teacher, so she used the knowledge package framework to approach him.

"What strategies do your students use to add fractions?" Ms. Garcia asked. Although she did not yet have an in-depth understanding of the curriculum at this grade level, she knew that this key question could at least begin a reflective conversation.

"I'm teaching the students how to make common denominators by multiplying the numerator and denominator by the same number," Mr. Delacorte answered.

"Right," answered Ms. Garcia. "I learned that traditional procedure when I was a child. But do our students understand why that works? What visual model can help them see that? And what other strategy can they use?"

These key questions allowed Ms. Garcia to engage the teacher in thinking more deeply about his work. If the teacher could not answer her questions, she was prepared to encourage him to find an additional strategy that would emphasize the meaning of numbers, perhaps by talking to other teachers, referring to the program support materials, or finding a book or online resource.

Knowledge packages are a simple tool for mathematics change: their simplicity allows schools to turn on a dime and realign their thinking about mathematics. Many schools have been surprised at the rate of change possible when teachers, coaches, and principals engage in discussions about knowledge packages. "I can't believe how much our school has changed in such a short time," is a comment that many a principal, coach, and teacher has made to us.

When teachers come to understand the relationships within knowledge packages, they find their voices. They learn what is important for students to understand, and they ask the right questions about how concepts, skills, strategies, representations, and mathematical language relate. When educators throughout the school ask these same questions, student experiences from class to class, from year to year, connect. Everyone is a link in the chain, and it takes time for links to forge. That forging happens when educators gain outside support and when they engage in school-based research about knowledge packages. The test of their strength is student success.

Learning Pathways

Although knowledge packages provide a useful structure for teachers to organize their knowledge about content, learning pathways are equally important. Learning pathways describe the mathematical landscapes that students typically pass through on their journey to developing complex mathematical concepts. Learning pathways are not necessarily linear, and students do not pass through this landscape of content in the same way or at the same time.

It is important for teachers to understand learning pathways for mathematics so they can understand how content builds, respond to common student misconceptions, and offer appropriate challenges to students who need them.

Examples of Learning Pathways

There is a sequential aspect to developing many number understandings. In order to develop various strategies for addition, students must be able to

- ° count;
- ° compare numbers; and
- ° decompose, or break apart, numbers and recompose them to solve problems.

Children can compare and decompose only those numbers to which they can count. Decomposing is the most difficult, since it requires students to recall three relationships between the whole and the two parts that create the whole.

Six-year-old Sarah can decompose 5 effectively, which means that when she sees 2 counters and knows that there are 5 in all, she also knows there must be 3 hiding under the upside-down cup. Since Sarah can easily predict when 1, or 3, or 4 counters are hiding, she can begin to use what she knows about 5 with larger numbers.

A child who knows how 5 is built (Figure 6.1a) will use that knowledge to understand how 10 is constructed (Figure 6.1b). Likewise, combinations of 10 help students with larger combinations, such as 20 and 100, which in turn help students learn how even larger numbers, such as 1,000 and 10,000, are built.

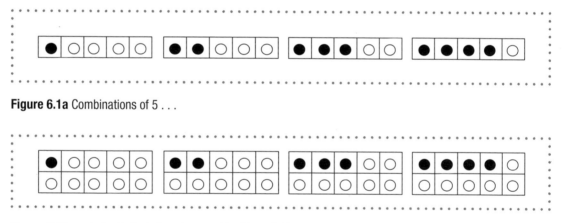

Figure 6.1a Combinations of 5 . . .

Figure 6.1b . . . help students learning combinations of 10.

Another learning pathway centers on how children learn story problems. It is important for teachers to distinguish between addition word problems where the result is unknown, and other stories where what is added, or the "change," is unknown. Addition stories with the unknown result typically are easier for students to solve, and should be presented first.

A story with an unknown result could go something like this:

Tanya had 5 books on her shelf. Then she put 3 more books on her shelf. How many books did Tanya have on her shelf then?

An equation for this story could be 5 + 3 = ____.
A representation for this story could be

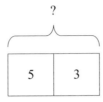

The same story with an unknown change could be

Tanya had 5 books on her shelf. Then she put some more books on her shelf, which gave her 8 books in all. How many books did Tanya put on her shelf?

An equation for this story could be 5 + ____ = 8.
A representation for this story could be

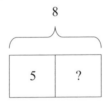

Students typically find the first story problem easier to understand and solve, so it makes sense to start with that kind of problem before working with unknown change problems. Principals, coaches, and teachers who then encourage students to grapple with both types of problems, and help them understand how they are alike and different, will help students become more powerful problem solvers.

Learning Pathways Help Teachers Respond to Student Misconceptions

Students make predictable errors as they work in any content area. Here are some examples:
°   Trent is a kindergartner who counts the same cubes over and over again without keeping track of what has already been counted.
°   Celia is a fourth grader who says that 2/6 is greater than 2/3.

In the same way that pediatricians are alert for common childhood illnesses in their patients, educators should be aware of common difficulties that students encounter as they study specific areas of mathematics. And in the same way that pediatricians understand the underlying mechanisms behind an ear infection and know how to treat it, educators need to understand the underlying reason for student misunderstandings in order to better respond to these errors. When teachers, coaches, and principals are knowledgeable about typical pathways that students take toward comprehending key mathematics topics, they can more effectively meet students' needs.

Although most teachers who have taught for several years have built up intuitions about ideas that are difficult for students, it is important that they move from general intuition about student errors to the ability to clearly articulate typical misconceptions that students have and to respond to those misconceptions.

The kindergarten teacher who sees that Trent does not keep track of the objects he has already counted should recognize that he likely views counting as a number-naming/object-touching activity rather than a tool for finding out "how many." In response, the teacher might thoughtfully select tasks that highlight the need for Trent to find out "how many," such as counting the crackers for snack time, and offer him tools for keeping track, such as deliberately counting and moving each item that has been counted.

When Celia said that 2/6 is greater than 2/3, her teacher should immediately consider the likelihood that she is responding to the numbers as if they were whole numbers rather than a ratio between numbers that compare parts to a whole. Celia may reason that, because 6 is greater than 2 or 3, the fraction 2/6 must be greater than 2/3. If the teacher's prediction is correct, the teacher must have a useful response in his or her repertoire. For example, the teacher might draw two equal bars and ask Celia to shade in each fraction, describe which part is greater, and then explain in her own words what 6 and 2 means in the first picture and what 3 and 2 means in the second picture. Although this single quick intervention does not guarantee that Celia will immediately gain a new understanding, a teacher who understands the underlying problem can help a child move toward that goal more quickly.

Other Advantages of Learning Pathways

Without a doubt children do not come in one-size-fits-all packages. Every teacher realizes that one lesson may be a perfect window on learning for one student but a firmly closed door to another. The same lesson may fence in yet another child, keeping him from exploring the more complex questions that he is excited about investigating. Learning pathways help teachers find ways to differentiate lessons for students who need additional challenges. For example, teachers can adjust a problem with an unknown result so that it becomes a problem with an unknown change.

Example of a "missing whole" problem:

Samira found 27 paper clips in a drawer and 14 paper clips in a box. How many paper clips did she have in all?

The same problem changed to an "unknown change" problem:

Samira found 27 paper clips in a drawer and some more paper clips in a box. She had 41 paper clips altogether. How many paper clips were in the box?

Ms. Conley is a first-grade teacher with a wide range of students, some who can count only to 10 and can't yet think of numbers in terms of wholes and parts, and others who can count to 100 and are ready to decompose 6.

She has a mixed-ability group of students at the same table, placing cubes along ribbons of different lengths. The struggling student counts the cubes and writes the numbers inside a small booklet. The more experienced student fits red and blue cubes along a piece of ribbon, and then records the number of red cubes, the number of blue cubes, and the total number.

Simple adjustments such as these are available to teachers who understand various learning pathways within mathematical topics. Learning pathways provide teachers, coaches, and principals with additional avenues for differentiation beyond the common teacher response of giving students more problems or changing the numbers.

Patterns in Content

When we drive the same way each day, our awareness of the journey fades and we suddenly realize that we have been on autopilot. When we change our route, the scenery snaps back into view, and we think of where we are in terms of where we want to be. Developing patterns in content provides us with a new reference point. Knowledge packages and learning pathways illuminate new possibilities to help educators make sense of this new world of mathematics.

The Principal's Perspective

I honestly have always found myself in a bind when I observe math lessons and need to talk to teachers about what I saw or need to give them feedback. I'm much more comfortable with literacy lessons, since I know more about decoding and comprehension strategies.

I just don't have that background in math. It's a tough thing to admit as a principal, but it's true—and really, it's not possible for anyone to know everything. So I find myself observing teachers' lessons for things that are "safe" for me, like whether the teacher used engagement strategies, or whether the pacing of the lesson matches what the textbook suggests. Although I know that engagement strategies are important, I'm not even sure that I should be checking whether the teachers teach each part of the lesson in the time frame that the teacher manual suggests. I just don't know enough about math and how to help the teachers.

Then one day my math consultant shared the idea of knowledge packages with me and showed me several examples of how they work in different math topics. I can't tell you how helpful that idea was! Now when I observe lessons using the knowledge package framework, I can better understand why they work, or even why they don't. Now I'm asking myself, and teachers, whether students can see the math. If not, then I know that visual models of the math are not there or students need to work with them more.

Knowledge packages made me much more aware of math language, and whether it's up in the classroom where the kids can see and refer to it, and whether the teachers and students use that math vocabulary throughout the lesson. I also watch for how big ideas are presented and whether the teacher is making connections between ideas.

Strategies are a big thing that I'm still making sense of. When I was a kid, and when I began teaching, there was only one way: the teacher's way. I remember trying to think for myself as a kid, and being told to just follow the teacher's way. So when I started teaching, I taught the very same way. Now I have to learn new strategies along with the kids, and I know that some of my teachers are in the same boat. But it was the knowledge package idea that helped me remember that there will always be more than one strategy, no matter what math topic is being addressed. So now I know to look for strategies and to talk to teachers about them.

One of my favorite parts of math lessons is watching the different ways that kids come up with to work on them. It's amazing to see what they do! The kids are proud of their strategies. It seems like they are in the driver's seat, and most of them really love math. That's a big change from how kids at this school used to feel about math.

This semester I'm trying to make time to teach in Ms. Moore's classroom as often as I can, which comes to about once a week. When we start a new unit, I talk to her first about the knowledge package for the topic that we're teaching. That gives me some guidance about what that unit is all about, and what we want the kids to know and do. Once I have a good sense of the knowledge package, the lesson planning is easier. And when we're actually teaching the lesson, I have a better idea about what we're chasing after.

The work that I do in Ms. Moore's class provides me with stories and examples that I use when I talk to other teachers about math. Knowledge packages have given me the courage to jump into teaching math. It represents the framework for understanding what's important in the math that we teach.

The Math Coach's Perspective

I met with our intermediate teachers and the principal yesterday for a half-day planning session. It was an amazing time for our team. I was very happy that they themselves decided to work on the important issue of math content, and that we accomplished so much in two hours. We have learned that strategies are a key part of any math topic that we teach. And now that the middle of the year is approaching and we have been working on many strategies with our students, we wanted to get more on the same page as a team and understand which strategies we make sure we all highlight.

We decided to begin with addition, and the more experienced teachers started to write sample strategies on the board. But as a facilitator I knew we needed to actually have everyone do the problems to ground the discussion in examples. Besides, I knew that all of us could use a chance to practice. I suggested that they write a sample problem on the board for all of us to solve, and that each of us use more than one strategy. That's how one of the best teacher discussions that I've ever had began! The teachers, principal, and I took turns going to the board to show how we solved the problem. Before long the board looked like Figure 6.2.

After everyone explained their thinking for each strategy, a question came up about strategy B: Why did 9 have to be subtracted? After a new teacher explained that "We added 9 too many so now we have to take it away," the conversation seemed to die out. But I wanted everyone to categorize the strategies, so I asked them whether any of the strategies were related. More talk followed, and some identified A and C as the same process but represented in different ways.

"I wonder how we can label strategies A and C," I said to the group. "And how are strategies B, D, and E different?"

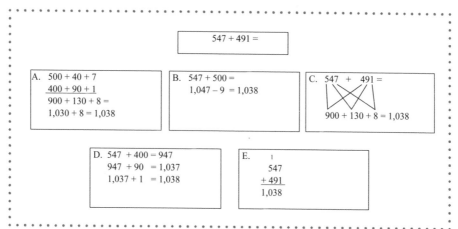

Figure 6.2 During a professional development session the teachers, principal, and coach came up with five different ways to solve a single problem.

A lively discussion ensued. Elizabeth summed up our conclusions: "In A and C both addends were broken apart, in strategy D one addend was broken apart, in strategy B one addend was changed to a landmark number, and E was the traditional algorithm."

I recorded our four categories on the board. "You talked about consistency over the grades," I said. "I think it would help our students if we all use the same category names for the strategies they use."

I also thought that naming the strategies would allow us to compare the categories for addition with those for subtraction, multiplication, and division.

Strategies for Addition
- Break apart both addends
- Break apart one addend
- Change an addend to a landmark number
- Traditional algorithm

Everyone was then ready to move on to subtraction, but I had one further question. "How explicit is each representation on the board?" I asked them. "Do any representations show thinking more clearly? Do any representations hide some steps in thinking? And which representations might be more helpful to students who are more fragile in their learning?"

Lynn, the principal, looked at strategy A thoughtfully. "You know, we could show where the expanded notation came from, and record this way. That might help the kids who have more difficulty thinking abstractly." She modified strategy A as shown in Figure 6.3.

Then Gene said, "That's right, and that reminds me of the partial sums strategy, which isn't up there. In my opinion it's a good bridge to the U.S. algorithm, since you can see why we 'carry.'" He added a new example, which he labeled F (Figure 6.4).

$$
\begin{array}{ll}
\text{A.} & 547 = 500 + 40 + 7 \\
& +\,491 = 400 + 90 + 1 \\
& 900 + 130 + 8 = \\
& 1{,}030 + 8 = 1{,}038
\end{array}
$$

Figure 6.3 The teachers agreed that this representation would most clearly illustrate place value, and would be a good initial strategy. Understanding learning pathways helps teachers determine what to do first.

$$
\begin{array}{lr}
\text{F.} & 547 \\
& +\,491 \\
& 8 \\
& 130 \\
& +\,900 \\
& 1{,}038
\end{array}
$$

Figure 6.4 The partial sums strategy is a bridge to the traditional algorithm.

"So you think that strategy F is a more explicit representation that might be more clear for some students," I said. "In which category does F belong?" Everyone agreed that for F both addends were broken apart.

Our discussions continued as we moved to other operations. But as a coach I was very pleased with the discussion and the learning that we did together. What I know is that the more clarity about mathematics content we bring to our teaching, the more our students will learn.

The Teacher's Perspective

I love teaching math this way! I get to peek into students' minds and see how they think. Even more rewarding is the chance to affect how they think. I've learned enough about math to know that we want students to be able to have multiple strategies for solving problems, and to use models such as hundred charts, number lines, and money models.

Yesterday the principal came in to introduce a visiting math coach to the kids, and she ended the introduction by asking, "Do you have any questions?" Mateo piped up with, "What's 25 x 25?" The principal laughed because that wasn't what she meant, but I took this opportunity to show the visiting coach how we help these third graders think about numbers. "Let's figure it out," I said.

The numbers were big for the kids, so I connected them to what they know: quarters. "How much is 4 quarters?" I asked them. "A dollar!" they said immediately. "So that's 100 cents," I said.

I continued helping them think. "Four 25s are 100, so 8 25s are _____," and the students chanted, "Two hundred!"

I continued, "And if 8 25s are 200, then 16 25s are _____," and the students filled in, "Four hundred!"

I wrote that on the board so the students could remember. "We've got 16 25s, so let's add on 4 more 25s, which is _____," and the students remembered that it would be another 100, "which gives us how much altogether?" The students knew we were up to 500.

We continued in that manner, and the students discovered for themselves that 25 x 25 = 625. I glanced at the visiting coach, who clearly was impressed. And I was pleased that the students understood how to break a complex problem down into smaller pieces.

That's what we're all about with the way we teach math. Students use what they know to figure out what they don't know. They know about money, and that helps them. Students learn to believe in their capabilities, and that makes them grow even stronger. We help them develop skills so that they can work more efficiently. And for these children, the sky's the limit!

Chapter 7
Patterns in Instruction

The way is long if one follows precepts, but short . . . if one follows patterns.

—Lucius Annaeus Seneca

We all have patterns that determine how we live our lives—we may make coffee first thing in the morning, or log on to our e-mail right when we get to work, or teach mathematics after reading. Many of our patterns are obvious to us; we've consciously chosen them because they help us be more efficient or effective. That morning coffee gives us the jump start that we need to get going, getting right to our e-mail helps us prioritize our schedule, and we teach reading first because that is the schoolwide schedule.

Other patterns, especially teaching patterns, may have crept into our lives subconsciously; we do them "just because." Giving pop quizzes every two weeks, or standing in front of the room as we teach, or arranging student desks in rows that face the front—that's how we've always done it. But do these patterns make sense?

All of us can remember our first year of teaching. We ourselves remember struggling with classroom management and the relief that flooded through us when we discovered the magic of positive reinforcement.

However, ineffective patterns of instruction can easily become the norm. We continue those patterns until, usually by chance, another teacher or a coach or a principal—or even a student—draws our attention to them. At that moment we have received a gift. We are awakened to a choice. We can choose to confront our own patterns—or not. Once we make a choice to question our patterns, we are in the realm of possibility.

The content area of mathematics compels educators to pry open the lid of that chest full of years-old patterns of instruction, to sift through them and examine them, using a new and perhaps unfamiliar lens. The Common Core State Standards for Mathematics require students to become deeply engaged in thinking, to persist in making sense of content, to apply their learning, and to reason critically and eventually abstractly. These goals must inevitably affect patterns of instruction.

The good news is that educators already have a sense of what these patterns are. Do you remember at least one college professor who lectured on and on, who filled the board with equations that made sense only to him, who moved from page to page, from chapter to chapter, seemingly oblivious to students' uncomprehending, glazed-over eyes? We do. However, when teaching mathematics we would never find ourselves in that position . . . or would we?

Even though we have examined our own teaching practices for longer than we care to admit, that bygone ghost creeps into our own teaching upon occasion. When he does, we usually find that we ourselves have inadvertently invited him in—by slipping back into old teaching habits. Immediately we readjust to better patterns, and that scary specter slinks away. When he does, we know that it's more likely that our students will learn and remember the meaning of fractions or decimals or polynomials. We know that good patterns of instruction improve the likelihood that learning will come to rest in students' long-term memories rather than flit into short-term memory and then escape.

When principals, coaches, and teachers research together what works for students and choose to make consistent instructional choices, authentic schoolwide discussions happen. Those discussions one by one, layer by layer, peel away old, ineffective habits and replace them with patterns so that not only do the most adept students find success, but *most* of the students do.

So what are these patterns of instruction? Why do they work? And how can principals, coaches, and teachers make sure that these patterns move from "That's a great idea!" to "I can't imagine teaching any other way"?

Pattern 1: Keep the Complexity

It's very clear to us that many of those glazed-over pairs of student eyes reflect not confusion so much as boredom. Most children like to learn and most want challenges, especially when a problem engages them. So give students interesting problems to solve, problems with clear, understandable questions but with answers that are not immediately obvious . . . and then let students solve them.

Notice that we said "answers." Problems that have more than one solution, and more than one way to get to those solutions, are especially engaging to students. Good mathematics problems are like a path up a hill that entices you to keep walking, to keep choosing your own twist or turn, a path that encourages you to keep exercising because you find it so interesting. Students are happy to exercise their "mental muscles" when they are given interesting problems to solve, when they are free to approach the problem in their own way, and when the problem challenges them but is doable.

Consider each problem below. Does each meet the criteria? If not, how might you change it?

° On this map, how far is it from Dallas to Houston?

° Solve 98 + 122.

° What is the perimeter of this figure?

12

3

Now compare the original questions with the following suggestions. Consider: Which versions are more engaging? Which versions have multiple solutions and ways to approach the solutions? And which do you think will more likely entice students into doing the mental work that will pay off in knowledge of basic facts as well as better math understanding?

° How many different ways can you find to go from Dallas to Houston? What might the advantage and disadvantage be for each route? Now find the shortest distance and write directions for taking that route.

° How many different ways can you solve 98 + 122? Which way do you think is most efficient? Why is it the most efficient for you? Explain your thinking in writing using mathematics vocabulary words, diagrams, and equations.

° Gina wants to make a garden 3 feet wide and 12 feet long. She wants to enclose it on all four sides. She has 16 feet of fence. Does she have enough fencing? How do you know? Explain your thinking in writing using representations, appropriate mathematics vocabulary, and labels.

"Keep the Complexity" is listed first in this chapter for no small reason. Educators in the United States tend to oversimplify content for students. The teacher habit of telling or leading students to answers is well documented. James Stigler and James Hiebert (2009), in *Closing the Teaching Gap,* note that when most teachers in the United States provide students with problems to solve, they very quickly revert to telling them how to solve the problems. Then teachers have students practice that one technique.

Numerous studies have shown that the most typical pattern of instruction that teachers use in the United States is this one:

°   Show students a procedure, have them practice, correct their errors.
°   Show students a procedure, have them practice, correct their errors.
°   Show students a procedure, have them practice, correct their errors.

This pervasive teaching pattern results in students simply waiting for teachers to tell them the answer. Students become very good at waiting, and train their teachers well. Many learn to be helpless at school, which seems to be one of the reasons that students do poorly on global assessments in mathematics. A common complaint among educators in the United States is that students "don't know how to think." We believe that students can think . . . if we would only let them.

In their analysis of the international Trends in Mathematics and Science Study, Stigler and Hiebert (2009) identify the teaching-by-telling approach as the main reason that students in the United States score significantly lower than those in high-achieving countries. After detailed analysis of videos of typical mathematics lessons in high-achieving countries, Stigler and Hiebert draw the following conclusion:

> Although teachers in the high-achieving countries employed a variety of strategies and routines, in every case these strategies were used to achieve a common learning experience for students. Czech teachers might lecture, and Dutch teachers might not, but their varied approaches all accomplished the engagement of students in active struggle with core mathematics concepts and procedures. It was this feature of teaching that we found common to the high achievers and missing in the United States. (34)

Basketball coaches understand the importance of complexity. They don't ask the players to practice only shooting baskets until their success rate is 90 percent. Instead they interweave some drills with practice games where someone is defending and there are complex plays and movement. Mathematics works the same way. Complex problems, which are the "game" in mathematics, help students understand why they need fluent skills, solid concepts, and efficient procedures.

Pattern 2: Keep the Math Visible

Most of us are visual learners. When students can "see the math," they better understand the relationships that are being discussed. "Now I see!" is what students often say, and it can literally be the case.

Before teaching a lesson, consider which visual models will most likely illustrate mathematical relationships. During lessons, consistently connect equations to that visual model. Teachers who explicitly and consistently make those connections improve the likelihood that struggling students or English language learners will comprehend what their classmates are saying and be able to participate in class discussions. Successful students who make those connections for themselves—and develop the habit of doing so—keep in mind the meaning of symbols.

Visual models do not in and of themselves communicate their meaning to students. Number lines can be especially elusive to children unless they have regular opportunities to create number lines, to use them to tell stories, to represent relationships on them . . . and to talk about what they see.

A class of second graders used a number line to illustrate a story about nine birds, four of which stayed in the tree and five of which left. Thomas showed his number line to Ms. Johnson (Figure 7.1a). "Did I do it right?" he asked.

"Take a look at the example on the board," Ms. Johnson suggested. "Does your number line show all the birds that stayed?"

Thomas looked hard at the number line on the board. "I think it's right," he said uncertainly. Even though he gazed at the model, Thomas didn't notice the details that mattered.

"Take your time," Ms. Johnson said. "Does your number line have the same type of information?"

A moment later his eyes brightened. "Oh," he said, smiling. "I'm missing the zero, and I didn't show how I made my jumps."

"What else?" asked Ms. Johnson.

"I didn't label what was happening, and I didn't count the jumps," Thomas continued.

"Good!" Ms. Johnson congratulated him. "Now you know what to do next."

Thomas gained a new understanding of using number lines to represent his thinking (Figure 7.1b).

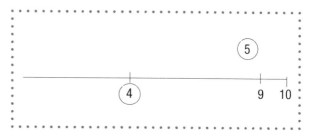

Figure 7.1a Before

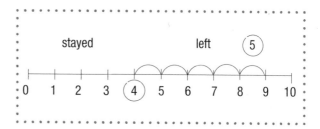

Figure 7.1b Ms. Johnson's questions helped Thomas realize how number lines function, so he revised his work.

Pattern 3: Bring Student Thinking to the Surface, Even If It's Wrong

"What do you think?"

"Why do you think that?"

"In what way do you agree or disagree?"

"Is that always true?"

"What did you do first? Why?"

These questions are the bread and butter of any math teacher, for they bring students' hidden thoughts to the surface. Once these ideas are on the table, right or wrong, they are ripe for examination by other students as well as the teacher. These questions elicit rich discussions where students talk to students and build on each other's thoughts. These questions create a mathematical community of learners who are curious to better understand how mathematics works and how they can use math to make sense of their world.

In Mr. Jacome's classroom, Jonathan shared his thinking about the polygon he drew on grid paper by drawing just on the grid lines (see Figure 7.2).

Jonathan said, "I think my polygon has the greatest perimeter you can have with an area of 11 square units. I noticed that shapes with a long perimeter are skinny, and this rectangle is the skinniest shape I could find." Mr. Jacome placed Jonathan's illustration on the document camera so that all the children could see it and better understand Jonathan's thinking. Mr. Jacome knew that it was important for all of his students—not just his English language learners—to refer to the visual model as Jonathan spoke.

Mr. Jacome did not immediately answer Jonathan with "You're right" or "That's not correct," because he prefers to have students take on that role.

"What do the rest of you think?" he asked the class. The students then shared their own polygons as evidence that Jonathan was correct—or not. Next Mr. Jacome facilitated a classroom discussion to help them sort out characteristics of polygons with the same area but different perimeters.

Wrong answers are opportunities to learn. A class of third graders shared their answers for how they solved 38 + 27. Ms. Calderon listed 55, 65, and 64 on the board. "How did you get your answer?" she asked. Justin shared how

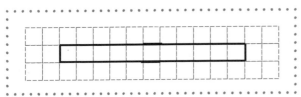

Figure 7.2 Perimeter: 11 + 11 + 2 = 24 units

he correctly got 65. Then Lashonda said confidently, "I'd like to explain how I got the wrong answer . . . 55. I added 30 and 20 and got 50. Then I added 8 and 7 and got 15. But I forgot about the 10 inside 15. . . . I just added 5 more."

Wrong answers are not unfortunate responses to be swept out of sight as quickly as possible. Instead they are food for thought. If Lashonda made that mistake, it's likely that other students did the same thing. Negative information—what doesn't work—is as important as positive information—what does work.

Pattern 4: Create a Rich Mathematical Environment . . . and Use It!

Classrooms have many teachers: the adult teachers and the students who teach each other. To us the classroom environment is still another teacher. Classroom walls are rich opportunities to display classroom-created posters to remind students about important ideas. A back shelf can turn into a museum of objects that weigh an ounce, a pound, and ten pounds, which students can heft when they need to recall how those benchmark weights feel. Math journals in desks, hundred charts at students' tables, and tubs of manipulatives on shelves allow students to independently find what they need, whenever they need it.

Carefully consider how to use your "prime real estate"—the space close to where you most often stand while teaching whole-group lessons. Contemplate how a math board (Figure 7.3) could support your teaching. Its large, accessible hundred chart can help students understand when their classmate is describing what happens when 10 is added to any number. A part/whole chart can illustrate how a student understands a word problem. A number line can help a child recall whether 32 is greater or

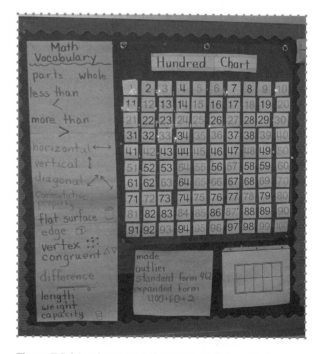

Figure 7.3 A teacher uses a classroom math board to leverage the environment to support the learning of mathematics.

less than 23. Just as a carpenter keeps the most important tools close at hand in a tool belt, so must we teachers maintain visual models at the ready during discussions, not only for our English language learners, but for all students.

A classroom environment rich with models can turn into wallpaper that disappears into the background, unless teachers and students consistently use it. "Feeding off the land" is how we describe students who use tools around them to answer questions. It is as important for teachers and students to refer to the classroom's mathematical environment as it is to create that environment in the first place.

Dr. Bill, principal of a large urban elementary school, found time to coteach a lesson with Mr. Jacobs, one of his most effective teachers. "I didn't realize exactly how important those math boards are," he said later, "until I saw three or four third graders walking up to the math board during investigation time. The kids were examining the fractions equivalency chart to answer a question—and Mr. Jacobs was able to keep talking with a student who was confused. Mr. Jacobs didn't have to say a thing to the students with the questions."

Pattern 5: Use Powerful, Predictable Patterns for Lessons

Mathematics lessons should have three parts: an introduction, an investigation, and a discussion. Lessons should always have these three parts—and *always* is not a word that we use very often. Lesson consistency does not turn teaching into a robotic, repetitive activity, but instead frees up teacher and student energy to focus on what is most important: the learning.

Part 1: Lesson Introduction
Lesson introductions simply orient students to that day's focus, how the lesson connects to previous work they have done, and why this idea is important. Lesson introductions can also build foundational knowledge whenever that knowledge is new and is necessary for the investigation. Whether the lesson involves a new topic or simply reviews previous work, students always benefit from some kind of introduction.

Lesson introductions can vary from a few minutes to as long as thirty minutes when teachers need to model or surround students with a new concept or skill. They are never just teacher-talk, but include real student engagement and deep thinking.

Part 2: Lesson Investigation

The middle, and usually longest, part of a lesson is the investigation. During the investigation, students are busily engaged in solving a problem or several problems, using what they know about a topic to figure out something that they don't know. Students might work alone, with a partner, or with a group, depending on the teacher's goals. Students may be engaged in a math workshop, where they choose from a variety of problems, or may all work on the same task.

During the lesson investigation, the teacher is usually not front and center. This frees the teacher to observe students, to support them in different ways, and to plan for the third lesson part: the discussion. If a student does not understand the problem being posed, the teacher makes sure it gets clarified.

Part 3: Lesson Discussion and Processing

The end of a lesson is prime learning time, when students share their ideas, and the discussions shape those ideas into stronger conceptual networks. Discussions are not the random "Who would like to share?" of our early years of teaching, but instead are focused and planned according to how the students responded to the investigation. Clear, targeted discussions are important.

For example, a teacher may "process" the discussion by having all the students practice a strategy that one student used to answer the question, "Does it always work?" Another teacher may create a classroom anchor chart listing strategies for identifying angle measurements, which can then stay on the wall to keep this important idea public. Still another teacher may use this processing time to model how to record a story problem with numbers and operations. Mr. Henry's fourth graders investigated this problem:

Claire had to swim for 2 hours during swim practice. She can swim 3 laps every 5 minutes. How many laps did Claire swim in 2 hours? Solve the problem in two different ways.

During the investigation, Mr. Henry noticed that Connie easily converted 2 hours into two groups of 60 minutes. She clearly comprehended how to decompose numbers and understood how repeated addition connected to multiplication. So Mr. Henry invited Connie to share her work with the class (Figure 7.4).

"Talk to your partner," he said to the students during the lesson discussion and processing. "Can you explain Connie's thinking in your own words?"

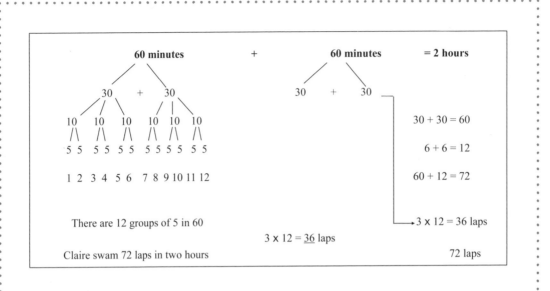

Figure 7.4 During the lesson discussion, Connie presented how she solved the problem.

Pattern 6: Keep the Kids Engaged

Our goal is to make sure that students are engaged throughout lessons. Even a short lesson introduction needs to engage students in the learning. Just as adults' minds quickly turn to the errands that must be done after school or the problems they are dealing with at home, so can children's minds stray from the topic at hand. Engagement strategies are key! Engagement strategies that we find most effective in mathematics include the following:

° Predictions, where students share the outcome they think will happen and then become invested in finding out if they were right

° Quick-writes, where students record what they think about a question

° Restating, where teachers ask students to restate what their partner said or what another student said to the class

° Choral response, where students answer a question or say a vocabulary word together

Using a small number of engagement strategies on a regular basis can be more effective than using reams of them. Selecting students to call on by pulling craft sticks with names from a can may be helpful in some circumstances; in others it could create a distraction. Watch the students for your evidence: Did the engagement strategy improve their focus and their ability to think?

While Ms. Frullo taught a whole-class lesson on addition and subtraction word problems, she kept an eye on how engaged her students were. She began her lesson with a quick-write by asking the students to write about how subtraction was different from addition. When Mary poked Carlos, Ms. Frullo moved closer to them, using the tool of "proximity." Before she asked Dennis to explain his thinking, she reminded the students that she might ask someone to repeat his good ideas to the rest of the class. And after Dennis answered the question, Ms. Frullo asked the partners to explain whether they agreed with Dennis or disagreed with him, and why. Ms. Frullo understands the importance of engagement throughout the lesson.

Pattern 7: Encourage Student Talk

Mathematics is often referred to as a language. It's true: math has its own vocabulary, its own syntax, and its own symbols. Math language rarely surrounds children at home, even in homes where literacy is prized. How many parents comment at dinner about the fascinating patterns that they encountered in multiples of different numbers that day? And how many families discuss prime factorization as they're riding in the car? Since the language of mathematics does not often surround children at home, teachers of mathematics need to see themselves as language teachers.

Students must become fluent in mathematical language both receptively (understanding when others speak) and productively (using the language themselves). Although this is even more of an issue for English language learners, all of us are mathematical language learners, because few of us were born into the language of mathematics. Mathematical language can exclude students from discussions and participation in the community of learners . . . or it can inclusively invite students in. Mathematical language can exclude students from primary instruction, or ideas can be made more comprehensible to them through the use of graphics, visual models, manipulatives, gestures, and language development techniques.

Vocabulary Development Strategies

Use vocabulary charts, where key mathematics vocabulary words and phrases are collected as a unit progresses.

Incorporate sentence frames to model the structure of mathematical sentences, especially for English language learners. To create a sentence frame, the teacher writes a math phrase with blanks and students substitute words to complete the sentence.

For example, A _____ is a polygon with ____ sides.
(triangle)   *(3)*

Reinforce students' use of high-level mathematical terminology by asking them to give a "thumbs-up" when someone says "sum" instead of "answer," or "I'm going to defend my answer" rather than "I'll tell you what I think."

Provide students with highlighters to mark each high-level mathematical word that they used in their writing.

Improve student comprehension of mathematical vocabulary by including both examples and nonexamples (Figure 7.5). Nonexamples clear up confusion and lead to deeper student understanding by identifying things that do not have that characteristic. When learning about polygons, for instance, students and teachers identify shapes that are not polygons as well as shapes that are polygons.

Gina said that polygons have to have straight sides, and most of you agree with her. Would anyone like to add to what she said? Are all figures with straight sides polygons?

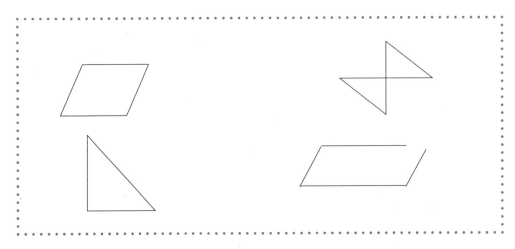

Figure 7.5   Example   Nonexample

From "Good Idea" to "Pattern"

"I used to use quick-writes, but I haven't done it in awhile," said Mr. Jordan.

"I know it's important to use engagement strategies, but I keep forgetting them," Ms. Linkhart mused.

We hear these comments from educators on a regular basis, and have even said them ourselves from time to time. We do understand the pressures on those in the teaching profession because we live with those pressures as well. Principals, coaches, and teachers are bombarded on an almost daily basis with the "latest and greatest" teaching idea. However, we believe that some instructional practices are so very important, so fundamental to student success, that they cannot be left to choice or chance. These ideas need to become teaching patterns that are used consistently by everyone in the school. These teaching strategies must move from "good ideas" to "classroom practice and research" to "instructional patterns."

So consider: How do you make changes in your own life? What motivated you to spend less money or exercise more or eat less? What helped you begin to recycle or learn to do your own taxes? What helped you remember to take out the garbage on Tuesdays or take your medication?

Many behavior specialists list these five elements that support changes in behavior:

1. The person has to *value the positive effect* that the behavior will have: If you spend less money, you can pay your bills and/or your savings will grow. If you exercise, you'll feel better and be healthier. If you recycle, you'll know that you're "helping the planet," and you'll feel good that you're not wasting precious resources.

2. The person has to understand at a gut level *what will happen if he or she doesn't change the behavior:* If you don't spend less, you won't be able to pay your bills and you won't be able to send your child to college. If you don't exercise, you'll have trouble sleeping and you'll be at risk of having a heart attack. If you don't recycle, the large-scale consequence is that landfills will fill up and taxes will rise as cities find it more difficult to deal with garbage.

3. The person needs to really *believe that they can make the change:* Role models who do these things, or friends who are also making these changes, are invaluable to the change process.

4. The person *needs a "trigger"* to make the behavior happen until it becomes automatic. Triggers might be a note inside the wallet that says "*Do you really need to buy this?*" or an exercise chart on the refrigerator, or a box beside the printer labeled "Recycling," or a spouse or friend who offers a friendly reminder.

5.   The person needs to "practice consistently" for a minimum of six *consecutive weeks* in order to override old patterns with new patterns. Think about the New Year's resolutions many of us make. When we break the cycle of working to maintain new patterns, we fall back into old habits. We find ourselves lounging in front of the television ("I'll just take a couple of days off . . .") and once again talking and talking at students ("I have too much to cover!"). Our old patterns grin slyly at us, and slip back into their comfortable places in our lives.

What might this look like in a school setting? Here are our best thoughts:

1.   Principals, coaches, and teachers need to value student success in mathematics. They need to know that mathematics taught well develops critical thinkers who can solve problems, make solid decisions, understand the effect of their choices, and be collaborative, informed citizens. Furthermore, students who understand mathematics and who have fluent skills are likely to do better on tests.

2.   Principals, coaches, and teachers have to truly understand that mathematics is no longer an option in our global, technologically based society—that doors to students' future opportunities will glide open or slam shut depending on their mathematical knowledge and skills. And, in our opinion, the future of our country and our world depends on developing critical thinkers.

3.   Principals, coaches, and teachers need to see other educators actually using these patterns, preferably with their own students in their own schools. When consultants model lessons at school sites, when teachers attend a summer institute and learn mathematics themselves through these patterns, or when teachers observe colleagues teaching this way at their own schools, the change suddenly looks doable. We hear comments such as, "My kids really got into the math!" "I didn't know my kids could do that!" "You taught my kids the same way you taught us at the workshop!"

4.   Principals, coaches, and teachers need "triggers" or reminders. A teacher decided to write "Turn to your partner . . ." on a neon yellow card and clip it to her math book. A principal decided to list these patterns of instruction on his door, and to offer five minutes of reflection on them at the beginning of each staff meeting. A coach used the patterns to write her lesson plans and debrief her coteaching and demonstration lessons.

5.   Principals, coaches, and teachers need to meet with each other for support. Reserving days to discuss your progress and bring the evidence of that progress keeps the fire burning bright. Working and meeting with colleagues lets them be a second set of eyes keenly focused on the changes you are practicing. This will give you greater clarity in your work.

Small but Consistent Steps

"How does the termite eat the tree?" asks the wise elder.

"One bite at a time," is the answer.

Our best advice to principals, coaches, and teachers who commit to improving their patterns of instruction is "*N* + 1."

Take that first step, *N*. Choose one new pattern, and intentionally make it a part of one day. And then another day. And then another. Notice how your students sit up straighter in their seats, see their eyes light up as they share their ideas, be aware of the effect of these changes: your students will focus better, do better, and remember better.

Once you take that first step, the next one will be easier, and the next one will be easier still.

Patterns in Instruction

Becoming conscious of our instructional patterns, in the company of colleagues and friends, we let go of established patterns.
We re-create who we are as principals,
                  coaches,
                        and teachers…
                       step
                             by step
                                    by step.

The Principal's Perspective

I'm glad we got some outside help to evaluate how we're teaching mathematics. We clearly have patterns of teaching math at our school. They just aren't producing the success that we need. Toward the end of last year, we were taking stock of where we were so we could plan for this year's professional development. The coach and I decided to watch math lessons in each classroom to see what we could learn. You can walk into a classroom and pretty quickly take a visual "temperature" of how the kids feel. In the first classroom the kids were slouched in their desks, and you could tell that their bodies were present but their minds really weren't. I almost had to stifle a yawn of my own. At the same time, I could see that Ms. Emmons had worked hard to prepare the lesson and was carrying out her plans. The problem was that her plans weren't producing the intended results. The coach and I know she cares deeply about our students and does plan her lessons. Even so, we are missing the mark.

It was really interesting to see how consistent our math culture was from classroom to classroom. Most lessons began with "Open your book to page ___." All the teachers showed the kids how to do procedures, and the kids practiced them. Kids quietly did their work while teachers helped the ones who were struggling. At the end of the lessons students quietly put their books away and got ready for their next subject.

The summer institute where the teachers, the coach, and I learned math with new patterns really pulled the rug out from under all of us. Suddenly the teachers could see that lessons needed to have three parts, and that the discussion at the end of the lesson was critical for their learning. Suddenly they understood that thinking deeply about fewer problems was more helpful than covering pages of examples. Suddenly they understood that intellectual struggle was part of the process, and that they needed to use these same patterns with their children.

We've been working on them this entire year. And I have to take the lead on this myself. I have to adopt these as my new patterns for teaching in the class where I work from time to time. What would it take for me to change my own teaching practices? That's where I need to start. That's where I need to go.

It's not that suddenly we're all experts or even as consistent as we'd like to be. But what is most important is that we're working on our patterns. We talk about these patterns during staff meetings. I share my struggles, and I'm honest about where I am in my own journey in making these changes. We all heard "small but consistent steps." I have to not only keep reminding myself, but take on the role of reminding others as well.

During Professional Learning Community time we talk about our changes. It is now clear to us that we do have control over our instruction. And we're seeing changes already. We're starting to hear kids talk about math. For the first time I'm hearing kids say, "I like math!" We're definitely on the right track.

The Math Coach's Perspective

I'm so glad that we are working with these patterns! What's interesting to me is how they help not just in math, but in literacy, too. Many are just good teaching practices. But somehow many of the teachers hear the message better when we apply it to math. Many of them talk about how they don't feel as confident teaching math; I think they're more open to new ideas in math than in literacy.

For my own teaching, I'm working on orchestrating the discussions at the end of the lesson. I tell teachers that, and when we coteach, we put our heads together as the students do the investigation. We plan how we want to focus the discussion, which students will share, and how we plan to make the new learning visible to the students—which visual model will help the students develop the concept we're working on.

It's true that our discussions don't necessarily take the path that we plan. That's the beauty of teaching—you never know what is going to happen, or what turn the discussion will take. But we do have a plan and a focus. We're a lot more clear about when and how to pull the conversation together.

Now that I'm being more explicit about what I'm working on in my teaching, I find that the teachers are talking about the same things. Most of us have abandoned the general discussion question "Who would like to share?" and have substituted more thoughtful, planned-out discussions.

During planning sessions with teachers, or lesson debriefings, I keep a list of these teaching patterns visible. The list is a trigger of its own, and it reminds all of us what we're aspiring to.

Patterns of Instruction
- Talk
- Questioning
- Engagement
- Vocabulary

It's exciting. We'll always be individuals who teach with different personalities, and our lessons will all look somewhat different as a result. But we really hope to get a lot more consistent with these patterns of instruction. I really believe that if we can internalize most of these patterns of instruction, our kids' lives will be much better. I really believe that our kids are depending on us.

The Teacher's Perspective

I have to tell you, my teacher training didn't prepare me for actually expecting students to make errors. I thought my job was to make sure that students did things correctly, so they never made mistakes. Now I see that mistakes are part of learning. If kids don't make mistakes, they probably are learning only at a surface level.

Last week I was talking with my kindergartners as they measured the long side of a picture book. And I couldn't believe what I heard! But in the end I was very glad that I did.

"It's 9 cubes," Rico announced as he pointed to the side of the book where he had carefully placed red cubes evenly, from end to end, with no gaps or overlaps. He sat back for a moment, satisfied, but then leaned forward to measure the same book again. But this time he used blue cubes of the same size. He carefully placed the blue cubes just as he had done with the red ones.

"Hmm," Rico murmured, his brow furrowed. "I got 9 again. That can't be right."

"Why do you think it can't be right?" I asked him.

"It's the blue cubes now," Rico replied.

Then another student, LaRonda, heard him and brought over different yellow cubes and set them alongside Rico's book, arranging them evenly, from end to end, with no gaps or overlaps.

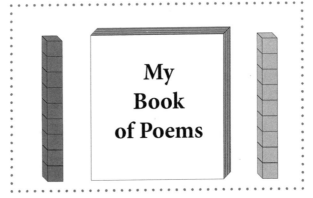

Figure 7.6 Rico is surprised that both cube trains have 9 cubes.

"I got 9, too!" she says, frowning. "That can't be right."

As I watched this, I had to ask myself, "What is going on?" Why did these children think there should be different numbers of cubes when they measured identical things with identical cubes of different colors?

But then I remembered how Piaget talked about conservation of number and conservation of space, and how young children attend to the arrangement of the counters rather than quantity—young children may think that if units are arranged differently, the total number should change. Maybe in this instance the students were focusing on the color of the units rather than the length of the units. I don't think they understand what measuring is, and why we're measuring.

If we create a context for measuring, if we create a scenario where the students have to communicate a length to a cousin who lives far away, will the students focus on length rather than color? I think I'll try that.

You know, I'm glad I realized that the some students think the measurement should change each time. Otherwise I would have blindly pressed onward with my measurement parade, only to find very few students behind me!

Chapter 8
Intentionality

The best time to plant a tree is twenty years ago.
The second best time is now.

—African proverb

Maybe you didn't plant that tree twenty years ago. Maybe you didn't begin planning for retirement in your twenties. And maybe you didn't start an exercise routine right when the doctor ordered you to. But when you do take that first step . . . that's the beginning of intentionality.

Taking the First Step

That first purposeful step toward meeting important goals that really matter can be the hardest step of all. What often keeps educators firmly planted in their present patterns of teaching is fear.

Teachers ask, "If I ask students to solve problems in more than one way, won't they get confused?"

Coaches wonder, "If the students can't memorize their multiplication tables, how can they think at a high level?"

Principals question, "Will their test scores get even worse than they are now?"

The answer is: "Asking students to think at a high level will help them understand why they need basic skills and practice using them." The follow-up question is: "What have you got to lose?"

Most schools' mathematics test scores suffer, and math scores frequently lag behind literacy scores. Typical school improvement efforts may bear little or no fruit. If so, rethinking approaches to mathematics program improvement is clearly required. It's been said that insanity is doing the same thing over and over again but expecting different results. Low mathematics test scores are a symptom of the need to seriously reexamine the "end" toward which teachers are working.

When students' test scores do meet the standards, a vision of even better possibilities is in order:

"Your students can *exceed* the standard."

"Your students can confidently solve problems in multiple ways."

"Your students can be competitive with students around the globe."

A Culture of "Can": Teachers

Intentionality is more than taking the first step. Intentionality means making sure that the newly planted tree is in the right spot, in the proper soil, and that it gets the appropriate amount of water. In education, intentionality means persisting when the students don't "get it" the first time. Intentionality means not teaching the same thing "louder and longer," but looking for a different way to reach the children. Because ultimately, intentionality is believing with all your being that your students can be successful at math and that you *will* find a way to make that happen.

There is often a difference—sometimes a narrow crack but sometimes a wide chasm—between what we say we believe and the true message that our actions and choices communicate about our beliefs. Several weeks after we did a lesson on alternative subtraction strategies in her classroom, a teacher said, "That day the kids really seemed to get it, but today they didn't remember it. They just don't retain things."

The teacher's comment was a window into her beliefs: her students can't learn math. She had done her part by teaching the lesson once, but the students forgot, and they were to blame.

To shift the discussion we asked, "Students are like all of us—it takes time for ideas to develop, especially when they are new to us. So what did you do to help the students remember? Did you keep the anchor chart on the wall for them to refer to?"

We looked on the walls and saw that this important reference had disappeared.

"Did you give the students opportunities to use the strategy in other situations or in math workshop?" we asked.

The teacher shook her head. "No."

If that same teacher had been looking through the lens of intentionality, she would have said something similar to this:

> "The kids really seemed to get it the other day, but today they didn't remember it. I wonder why. What can I do to help them retrieve that experience, get even better at it, and eventually add that strategy to their personal toolbox?"

Teachers with an intentional framework naturally move to brainstorming sessions about solutions. Teachers with an intentional framework might consider ideas such as real-world application problems, ten-minute skill reviews, and games that could help the children not only remember, but also become more fluent with that alternative subtraction strategy. Teachers with an intentional framework believe that students *can* achieve and ask themselves this important question: "What will it take?"

However, at that moment this teacher believed that the children were at fault.

We understand that even teachers with the best aspirations for children can tumble into a downward spiral and fall into the blame game. Keeping that in mind, we took a positive approach with this teacher and brainstormed possible instructional responses with her.

At the end of our discussion, the teacher began to talk about the "next steps" she was going to take. We made a note to follow up on her plans, because our role is to be her support, her second set of eyes and ears, her source of accountability, and her reminder of what is possible for children to achieve.

We were confident that her students would be more successful, and that our next discussion would be a celebration of how these children could learn math effectively. On the other hand we also realized that if the teacher consistently chose to blame the children, the principal might have to intervene.

A Culture of "Can": Coaches

Coaches need the same level of support and accountability as teachers do in order to grow in their roles.

"Teachers aren't implementing their mathematics program with fidelity," commented a coach. "Their lessons don't always come from the book."

In return we questioned, "What does fidelity mean? Does it mean to always follow a math program that someone who doesn't know your students created, or does it mean consistently reflecting on what students do as a result of our decisions and adjusting accordingly?"

Intentionality aims at the core of what is important: coaches supporting teachers as they make sense of the curriculum and how to teach it most effectively. When coaches are intentional about working side by side with teachers in classrooms, their language reflects this position. When we hear coaches saying "your" students or "your" lesson when they talk to teachers, we often make some suggestions: "Calling them 'our' students might open a better line of communication." "Working alongside teachers turns it into 'our' lesson."

Ms. Peterson, a coach new to her position, sat down beside us, clearly struggling with her emotions. "I don't know about our sixth-grade teacher, Ms. Volker," she said with frustration. "She just lectures the students no matter what I do! I don't think she's a good fit for our school."

We listened to her well-intentioned words, and saw the lines of fatigue in this hardworking coach's face. At the same time, we knew that Ms. Volker worked equally hard, determined to have her students pass her class with the knowledge and skills they needed for middle school.

After acknowledging the coach's frustration, we moved the conversation away from scarcity, back to abundance, away from deficits to possibility. "Why do you think Ms. Volker lectures so much?" we asked.

"She's just 'old-school,' " Ms. Peterson said.

We smiled, remembering our own pasts. "Well, once we were 'old school,' too, and we taught just like her." We paused to let that idea sink in. "Teachers like us have to see the proof before we are convinced. What if we propose a little research study to her? We'll do several lessons in her class on angles using pattern blocks and problem solving. After she sees how engaged her students are, and how well they understand angles, she may very well be open to the possibility of other effective ways of teaching."

Teachers are motivated by success just as students are. Keeping possibility in view, and building on the evidence of success, is the essence of intentionality in coaching. Sharing the ups and downs with a colleague, and having a fellow traveler to consult with, commiserate with, and then celebrate with, makes the learning indelible.

A Culture of "Can": Principals

As with teachers and coaches, principals need support and accountability to grow as leaders.

"My principal is a good manager, but she doesn't know classroom instruction." This comment circulates throughout many schools.

It is important to remember that principals started out as teachers, and once may have complained about their own principals. Our view is that teachers and coaches should help principals take on that often-risky role of participating in instructional decisions. When teachers and coaches intentionally involve the principal in planning sessions, the principal will grow in his or her knowledge of mathematics and instruction, and will be more likely to share in the responsibility for the outcome of that plan.

"We'd like you to join us as we score our end-of-unit assessments," Mr. Mason said to his principal. "The third-grade teachers would really like your ideas about how to up the ante with our students' work." Once the principal joined in that brainstorming session, she engaged the second-grade teachers in a similar conversation. With principals, just as with teachers and students, success breeds confidence, and then confidence breeds more success.

In our work with schools we invite principals to participate in planning sessions and lesson debriefings, in examining student work and in struggling with what to do with Anthony, who still doesn't understand how to use a number line. We ask principals to pick up that marker in classrooms and try out an engagement strategy, or to come up with ways to challenge Amanda, who finishes her work quickly and easily. Every role in the school has its challenges, and principals need the same support as teachers and coaches. Everyone wants to be successful at what they do, including principals.

When principals, coaches, and teachers assume the best about each other, a culture of "can" turns into a culture of "will" and finally transforms into a culture of "We're doing it!"

Intelligence Is Malleable

Many teachers, principals, and coaches unwittingly put up their own roadblocks of impossibility: they believe, either consciously or subconsciously, that genetics determines student success in school. On a regular basis we work with kind, dedicated, caring teachers who make comments such as, "Our kids can't solve problems" or "Our kids can't think."

Why might this be? To give them credit, these teachers have plenty of what they interpret as "evidence." They have repeatedly opened their bag of teaching tricks, and they've used them all. So when, frustrated, they peer once again into that bag, they find it empty. They inevitably conclude, "I've been working hard. I've done all that I can. It must be the kids." The teachers have all the "evidence" they need.

Teachers teach within a national culture that for the most part believes in the "math gene." Many adults attest that a few special people are good at math, and that they are born that way. They believe that most of us "can't do math," and it is not uncommon to hear an adult make that statement clearly, boldly, and sometimes even proudly. On the other hand, people who can do math may be considered outside the norm and perhaps even a little suspect. Movies and television often portray people who are good at math as being out of touch and having little fashion sense—sporting bad haircuts, wearing unfortunate plaids or too-short pants—and sitting home alone on Saturday night.

In reality, there is no math gene. Most people can be successful at math—and of course fashion sense is independent of number sense. Success in mathematics is largely the result of experience, in the same way that learning what clothes fit your particular frame may depend on the experience of having a good friend give you feedback on your choices of outfits.

Students need to be told—over and over—that being good at math is the result of work. Students need to be told—over and over—that practice is the key to success. Then students need to recognize how their work pays off. Are they fluent with more facts? Do they use the correct operation more often? Do they get more accurate answers when they subtract? Do they understand more geometry vocabulary?

In schools student success breeds more success, and over time, that success compounds and grows. Eventually school norms change, so that being good at math is something that kids strive and work hard for. When math becomes an important part of social capital for students, being "smart" at math is valued and cool.

Student Intentionality

A culture of "can" is not created by teachers and principals alone; it comes about when students themselves discover that they can be successful. Raoul, a fifth grader, slumped in his seat as his teacher announced another multiplication timed test. Raoul's expression was hopeless, and seemed to say, "I didn't pass the test last week and I won't pass it this week—or any other week either." Raoul saw evidence of his failure in his folder of weekly tests covered with red checkmarks. Even though Ms. Smith fit an extra tutoring session for him into her busy schedule, Raoul was still confused by multiplication.

But one Monday Ms. Smith came to class with a smile on her face. "Raoul," she said, "I know what will help us over this hump." An online course focused specifically on fluency with basic facts had given her ideas about how to break down Raoul's seemingly impossible task into related chunks.

Once Raoul saw how the multiples of 2—which he did know—would help him with his 4s, he began to breathe more easily: there was some hope, he discovered, that he could learn his multiplication tables.

Next Ms. Smith helped him use his 2s to help him with his 3s, by adding just one more group. A little at a time, Raoul began to taste success, and he learned to like it. That little bit of success encouraged him to practice more, and of course the more he practiced, the better he became. After three weeks Raoul still had trouble with some of the multiples of 7, but he looked with satisfaction at that week's timed test: he had scored 80 percent.

Part of the teacher's task is to help students become intentional learners. Teachers, principals, and coaches must work together to instill a sense of competence and urgency in their students.

Educators must

Figure 8.1 This second-grade teacher continually conveys to her students that getting smart comes from working hard, and that all of her students can go to college.

- convey the message over and over again that "Smart is not something you are; smart is something you get": *"It's possible."*
- explicitly help students become personally invested in their own learning until they understand that success will have a positive effect on their choices today, next year, and throughout their lives: *"I want."*
- help students set achievable goals and track their own movement toward success: *"I can."*
- share examples and stories from this class that illustrate the payoff of effort: *"I will."* (See Figure 8.1.)

Being Present—A Framework of Consciousness

You can't be intentional about something you can't observe. Being intentional requires teachers, coaches, and principals to be present in the moment, conscious of children, children's thinking, and the goals they have in mind.

How often have you found yourself driving, looked up, and suddenly realized that you don't know how you got to your destination? You recall backing out of your driveway, but you have no recollection of the left turn that you made, or your stop at the red light. You were on autopilot, your subconscious mind taking over the driving while your conscious mind was focused on something else.

"But I could never be on autopilot in the classroom!" you might protest. "I'm present for the children!"

But in fact it is normal for our attention to wander to the many demands that cry out for our attention, to the anxieties that sit on our shoulders and whisper in our ears:

Ricky's answer is wrong again, and it doesn't even make sense! How will he ever do well on the state test?"

"The math period is almost over, and we haven't even finished the second unit. I'm falling farther and farther behind."

"Sophia didn't bring her homework—again."

The best of us experience these concerns and even doubt our abilities as teachers, coaches, and principals. The key is to not lose ourselves in those anxious thoughts, but to acknowledge that things are not as we would wish and move back into consciousness and possibility: Ricky is doing better than he was, your students are digging deeply into the ideas in this math unit, and Sophie is probably doing the best she can, given the issues she deals with at home.

A framework of consciousness asks us to maintain our focus on what we can control. Consciousness allows us to be aware of the new instructional patterns that we are honing to replace the old ones. Consciousness allows us to glimpse the old patterns that continually try to creep into our teaching, unwelcome and unannounced. Consciousness allows us to acknowledge our lapse and remind us of where we want to be.

Suggestions for Intentionality

1. Keep the standards high. Kids know when you believe that they have the ability, and more often than not they rise to your expectations. The *Mi Hijito Syndrome* (my little child) is a term we use in the Southwest for teachers who show their affection for their students by making the work too easy. Kindness is not always kind.
2. Each minute is important. We teach from the first day of school to the last day of school, and we "chase after" key mathematics ideas throughout the day. Even lining up for lunch or preparing to go home provides teachers with chances to have students name even numbers or count by multiples of 10.

3. Keep the lesson pace moving forward. At the same time, be aware of the times when students need thinking time, or chances to talk to a partner or their group. Respond to the students as a coach or piano teacher would: label positive improvement, encourage students to flex their intellectual muscles, and require all students to participate.

4. Provide meaningful practice so that students can become fluid, fluent thinkers.

5. Design lessons with high-level ends in mind, and continually check that the students understand. Asking students to do a "quick-write" about what they already know about a topic at the beginning of a lesson easily lets educators identify what learners bring to the lesson. "Closing problems" at the end of a lesson are a window into what students know at that point. Be methodical about the three-part lesson. (See Chapter 7: "Patterns in Instruction.")

6. Require high-quality work from students and celebrate high-level thinking. If vocabulary words are in the classroom environment, students should spell them correctly. If students are capable of using high-level strategies, they should use them.

7. Teacher meetings and planning sessions end with "next steps" and include "by when" those steps can be expected to happen. And make sure that meetings always begin with a check-in about previous "next steps."

8. Be intentional about who is at the table when decisions are made. Many schools work in scarcity, including "the good teachers" in decisions and excluding others. In reality, diversity challenges us to consider other perspectives and come up with better solutions. Valuing differences promotes a healthy school culture based on respect for differences. Abundance requires the knowledge that "excellence" happens when all of us—principals, coaches, and teachers— are great at what we do.

Remember that small steps and changes are fine but they must be consistent and intentionally planned. The steps that teachers, coaches, and principals take may vary by timing, they may differ in details, and they may progress down paths that are unique to each individual. The critical element, however, is for all teachers, coaches, and principals to aim toward the agreed-upon North Star that guides them in the same direction, toward the "end" they all have in mind (see Figure 8.2).

Figure 8.2 It is not always clear what the "end in mind" should be. Two classroom teachers examine student work to identify high-quality work for their grade.

Intentionality

Although it's true that the best time to plant a tree was twenty years ago . . .

and the best time to begin partner talk was when the students were in kindergarten . . .

and the best time to allow the students to solve a problem with different strategies was at the beginning of the year . . .

. . . the second-best time is now!

The Principal's Perspective

I just observed a lesson in Ms. Logan's classroom that had some wonderful aspects to it—the students were engaged, and there was a very friendly teacher/student relationship—but what was lacking was intentionality on the part of the teacher. It seemed that Ms. Logan was going through the lesson steps without expecting the students to achieve the goal of the lesson. In fact, I wonder whether she was clear herself about what that goal was.

The first graders were playing a sorting game called Guess My Rule. Each student sorted a set of shapes and then had his or her partner try to determine the attribute that the student had used to sort them. Although the students enjoyed this game, Ms. Logan never brought them together afterward for a discussion about the strategies they were using to figure out the rule. I know that when I cotaught with Ms. Lee, I worked hard to make sure that each lesson had a discussion component. I think I'll share my story with Ms. Logan, and ask her to think about how a discussion would have helped her first graders. Without the discussion, the students who used random strategies were left at that level, and they never got to see any other way to work.

I've been thinking about other things that I try to do as a principal to help teachers become more intentional:

1. When we begin planning a lesson together, I ask, "What do we want students to know and be able to do by the end of the lesson?" This question based on "backward planning" creates the habit of keeping the end in mind. To answer this, the teacher must look at the lesson objectives and synthesize all the objectives into what is most important for the students to learn.

2. Next I ask, "What do students need in order to do that?" We talk about the concepts and skills, strategies, visual models, and vocabulary that are necessary.

3. During the planning session we talk about how we'll find out whether the students learned what we wanted them to learn.

4. During the planning we address why this concept or skill matters—how it fits into the larger picture of what children need to know. For example, when I debriefed with the teacher about sorting, we talked about how sorting is how children make sense of their world, but that it is also fundamental to gathering and analyzing data; graphs display information that has been sorted so that it's easier to compare.

5. In the middle of lessons that I teach alongside teachers, I ask them where we are in terms of the intentions that we had at the start. I ask, "Where do we see the evidence of the learning we had hoped for at this point in the lesson?"

6. When we debrief lessons, I have sticky notes available. Both the teacher and I write notes to ourselves to remind us of our next steps, either for the next day or when we do the same lesson another year.

I also like to share with teachers my own stories—that it took me two years to stop immediately answering student questions. Being "the sage on the stage" was a really hard habit for me to break. That pattern was so persistent that it took me two years to replace it with asking questions. Maybe I'm slow. But I persisted.

I had to remain alert for the pattern I was trying to replace. I'd find myself slipping into it, and I'd tell myself, "Darn! There it is again! Next time I'll . . ." And I'd think of what I wished I had done instead. I gave myself a percentage: I'm 40 percent there. I'll feel confident when I'm at 80 percent. Eventually I found my habits changing, and I asked more questions and gave students think time. My teaching has changed a lot and is still changing as we speak.

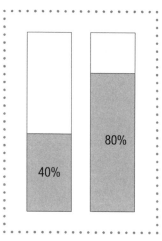

Figure 8.3 Giving yourself a percentage for consistency with new practices brings consciousness to the change process.

The Math Coach's Perspective

I've been thinking about the teachers at my school. We have had a big push this year toward using engagement strategies such as "think, pair, share" and "choral response" (where the students repeat words or respond to an answer as a group).

And, although a few teachers have incorporated these tools into their teaching, the majority have not.

"I know these teaching strategies are important," Ms. Hastings confided in me. "But I forget to use them. I get so wrapped up in my teaching that they don't occur to me." I was pretty sure that other teachers at my school shared Ms. Hastings' perspective, even though they really care about doing a good job. I knew that it was up to me to find a bridge to help instill these habits.

During a planning session I asked the fourth-grade teachers to explain why we would want to make these ideas consistent habits.

"The kids pay attention better," said Ms. Hastings.

"And they'll remember what we're teaching better," added Mr. Palacios.

"Those are both good reasons to make these strategies part of our regular practice," I said. "One way to look at it is that they help the ideas move from short-term memory to long-term memory. I often hear teachers say that their students don't remember what they've learned. These strategies can help enormously."

We planned to coteach a lesson, but I decided to add the twist of "whisper coaching," where I whisper suggestions to the teacher and the teacher whispers suggestions to me. I looked at Ms. Hastings. "Why don't you be in charge of vocabulary," I suggested to her. "Get a piece of butcher paper, label it 'Geometry Vocabulary,' and list the vocabulary that the students need to learn. And, during the lesson, use the vocabulary yourself and make sure that the students repeat it and use it in context. Be sure to have the students use the vocabulary. If I'm teaching at that moment and you see a good opportunity for students to use the vocabulary, just signal to me to remind me. And if I see some chances for you to do that, I'll do the same for you. We call that whisper coaching, and we can do that for each other."

"Should I list the vocabulary before the lesson or add it during the lesson?" Ms. Hastings asked me.

"Great question!" I responded. "I've struggled with that question myself. My preference is to add the vocabulary during the lesson as it comes up, so that the students participate in creating the chart. But it can work either way. You decide what makes sense to you."

Then I turned to Mr. Palacios, who was also going to be present at the lesson. "Why don't you be in charge of using 'think, pair, share,'" I suggested. "Make sure that we have students talk in partners whenever important points come up in the lesson." We discussed what those important ideas would be.

Then Mr. Palacios confided, "I have trouble figuring out what to have students talk about." His comment made sense. The questions now come more easily to me, but I hadn't realized that they could be difficult for teachers to come up with. So together we devised several questions that work in multiple situations: "Do you agree or disagree with what was said? Why?" and "What other way can you solve the problem?" My favorite was an all-purpose question that the teachers could use in almost any setting: "Tell your partner your answer and explain how you know it's right." I suggested to the teachers that we model for the students what partner discussions looked and sounded like.

I have to say that this lesson was one of the most exciting ones I've ever cotaught with teachers. Ms. Hastings did an outstanding job with vocabulary, and Mr. Palacios got very good at using "think, pair, share." It was interesting to watch both teachers begin somewhat awkwardly and then become much more confident by the end of the lesson. It reminded me of watching someone learn how to ride a bike—at first a bit wobbly and then pedaling smoothly away.

"That was really fun!" Ms. Hastings said, smiling. "I learned a lot today."

"I can see that it's possible for me," Mr. Palacios added. "The kids got really good at talking to each other. They liked it, and I think they'll really remember what we did." I acknowledged their success, but asked how they will be sure to continue using "choral response" and "think, pair, share." The teachers decided to keep a tally of their use of those engagement strategies during the coming week. I said I would check in with them on Friday to see how it went.

I really think I'm learning about how to help teachers be more intentional. I think of the times that I got frustrated when teachers didn't immediately use the good ideas I shared with them. Now I know that I have to help them bridge from theory to practice.

The Teacher's Perspective

Here I was, with just six weeks left in the year, wondering if I would have to retain one of my first graders, KaNaya. I hate to keep any of the kids back, but I especially felt bad about KaNaya. She's such a sweet little girl, always smiling, always working hard. She's so eager to learn, so eager to please.

But that day I asked KaNaya what $8 + 1$ was, and she wrote 5 on her whiteboard. It hit me that this kind of response wasn't unusual for her.

"What should I do?" I asked myself. "Here's a little girl who wants to learn and who gets support from her parents, but her number sense just isn't there."

That's when I heard the voice that I hate, sitting on my shoulder, telling me to give up. "Maybe she can't," the voice whispered. "After all, KaNaya is homeless and her family moves from shelter to shelter. How can that not affect her?"

Then I thought back to when I started this job: I firmly believed that all children could learn. At that moment I resolved to turn that negative voice into a call to action: If KaNaya wasn't getting it, I had to change. I had to try something different. And it was March! It would have been better if I had intervened earlier, but I hadn't, so the second-best time was now.

I began keeping KaNaya in the classroom during my planning time while the other kids went to the library and music. We had to go back to what the class had done in October and get back to concrete models—doing story problems about things that she loved.

KaNaya loves the ocean, so we did story problems about whales and starfish and mermaids. I would tell her the story, and then she'd tell it back to me. Then KaNaya would show the story with cubes, and she'd write the number sentence that told the same story.

KaNaya also adores eating Hot Chips, so we did stories about them. I told KaNaya, "You put 5 bags of Hot Chips in the grocery bag. Your mom saw you and so she took out 4 of them."

"Ooh! I love Hot Chips!" KaNaya would squeal. And she'd hunker down to try to figure it out.

Then I witnessed a turning point. KaNaya began solving +1 problems quickly! Then +2 problems became easy. The pieces started to fit together for KaNaya—those other math concepts the class had been learning began to make sense to her.

Yesterday I gave KaNaya a story problem about penguins, and she immediately wrote the number sentence $5 + 3 = 8$.

"Can I do the commutative property?" KaNaya asked. I realized that this level of problem had become boring for her, and she was looking for a way to ramp it up. She wrote $3 + 5 = 8$.

"Two commutative properties!" she said, laughing.

As I look back, I realize that what changed was not KaNaya, but me. She is still a child of poverty and may deal with huge issues throughout her childhood. But because I replaced that doubting voice with a sense of possibility, KaNaya has not only caught up to the class, but found confidence in math. Because I maintained my belief in KaNaya's ability to learn, I pushed forward. I made math personal, relevant, and interesting to her. KaNaya just needed to have her training wheels on longer, and I found the time and space for her to do what she needed to do.

That's the hardest thing about teaching—the voice that says you've done all you can. That voice has become my cue to find another way and another time to relentlessly pursue success for all my children. That voice is my call for action. It's never just the students. Never.

Possibilities for children have to start with all of us. The small steps that I continually take along with my coach, my principal, and other teachers over time have led to big changes. At first we hardly noticed them. Then one day, as we were watching our students in the midst of a true mathematical argument, presenting their unique ways for solving the same problem, respectfully disagreeing with each other, and then justifying their own thinking, we realized just how far we've come. Together we have made a lasting difference in the lives of our children.

References

Chapin, Suzanne, Catherine O'Connor, and Nancy Canavan Anderson. 2009. *Classroom Discussions: Using Math Talk to Help Students Learn.* Sausalito, CA: Math Solutions.

Collins, Jim. 2001. *Good to Great: Why Some Companies Make the Leap . . . and Others Don't.* New York: Harper Business.

Confer, Chris. 2005. *Teaching Number Sense: Grade 1.* Sausalito, CA: Math Solutions.

Covey, Steven. 2004. *Seven Habits of Highly Successful People.* New York: Free Press.

Fosnot, Catherine Twomey, and Maarten Dolk. 2001. *Young Mathematicians at Work: Constructing Number Sense, Addition and Subtraction.* Portsmouth, NH: Heinemann.

Fullan, Michael. 1993. *Probing the Depths of Educational Reform.* London: Falmer.

Garmiston, Robert J., and Bruce M. Wellman. 1999. *The Adaptive School: A Sourcebook for Developing Collaborative Groups.* Norwood, MA: Christopher-Gordon.

Hiebert, James, Thomas P. Carpenter, Elizabeth Fennema, Karen C. Fuson, Diana Wearne, Hanlie Murray, Alwyn Olivier, and Piet Human. 1997. *Making Sense: Teaching and Learning Mathematics with Understanding.* Portsmouth, NH: Heinemann.

Lipton, Laura, and Bruce Wellman with Carlette Humbard. 2003. *Mentoring Matters: A Practical Guide to Learning-Focused Relationships.* Sherman, CT: MiraVia.

Ma, Liping. 1999. *Knowing and Teaching Elementary Mathematics: Teachers' Understanding of Fundamental Mathematics in China and the United States.* Mahwah, NJ: Lawrence Erlbaum.

Richardson, Kathy. 1999. *Developing Number Concepts: Addition and Subtraction.* Parsippany, NJ: Dale Seymour.

Stigler, James W., and James Hiebert. 1999. *The Teaching Gap: Best Ideas from the World's Teachers for Improving Education in the Classroom.* New York: Free Press.

———. 2004. "Improving Mathematics Teaching." *Educational Leadership: Improving Achievement in Math and Science* 61 (5): 15.